Tiferet

FOSTERING PEACE THROUGH LITERATURE & ART

Printed in the United States of America

ISSN: 1547-2906
ISBN-13 978-0692106914
ISBN-10: 069210691X

Tiferet

SPRING/SUMMER 2018

FOUNDER & PUBLISHER
Donna Baier Stein

EDITOR-IN-CHIEF
Gayle Brandeis

MANAGING EDITOR
Lisa Sawyer

POETRY EDITOR
Adele Kenny

SUBMISSIONS EDITOR
Jeremy Birkline

ASSISTANT EDITORS
Kristen Turner
Mary Garhart
Pamela Walker

CONTRIBUTING EDITORS
Nancy Lubarsky
Priscilla Orr
Bob Rosenbloom

DESIGNERS & ILLUSTRATORS
Donna Schmitt
Monica Gurevich-Importico

INTERNS
Courtney Harler
Rebecca Kuder
Tate James
Aaron Schwartz
Kate Halse
Kelly Hobkirk
Anne Hoffnagle
Anu Mahadev
Natalie Hirt
Teri Fuller Rouse

COVER ART
"Spring's Calling" by Sandra Erbe

Tiferet

SPRING/SUMMER 2018

TIFERET TALK ON BLOG TALK RADIO:

HOST
Gayle Brandeis

EXECUTIVE PRODUCER & FOUNDING PUBLISHER
Donna Baier Stein

SENIOR PRODUCER
RJ Jeffreys

ASSOCIATE PRODUCER
Udo Hintze

TIFERET CAN...

Inspire you to write

Connect you to a global community

Lead toward peace in you and in the world

▶ **SUBSCRIBE TODAY** to enjoy beautiful, inspiring poetry, fiction, creative nonfiction, interviews and visual art from some of today's best writers.

PAST CONTRIBUTORS INCLUDE:

ROBERT BLY	JEAN HOUSTON	ROBERT PINSKY
RAY BRADBURY	STEPHEN DUNN	ED HIRSCH
ILAN STAVANS	ALICIA OSTRIKER	JANE HIRSHFIELD

and so many more . . . Pulitzer Prize winners to newcomers!

You are welcome to submit your own work (*poems, stories, essays, interviews and visual art*) for us to consider for publication. We also run an annual Writing Contest and award $1500 in prizes.
More details can be found at www.tiferetjournal.com.

Tiferet: Fostering Peace though Literature & Art is published twice a year in print and digital formats. We read only electronic submissions made through our website submission feature; submissions made through email attachments or by postal delivery will not be considered.

SUBSCRIPTION INFORMATION

One Year Subscription	$21.95 (two print or digital issues)
Two Year Subscription	$39.95 (four print or digital issues)
Three Year Subscription	$59.95 (six print or digital issues)
Single Print Issue	$14.95 + $3.15 S&H

U.S. currency (cash or check) and Visa, Mastercard, American Express are accepted. For international delivery, extra charges will apply. Please inquire.

ALL OTHER CORRESPONDENCE MAY BE DIRECTED TO:

Tiferet Journal
211 Dryden Road
Bernardsville, NJ 07924

editors@tiferetjournal.com
www.tiferetjournal.com

VISIT TO ENJOY CURRENT SPECIAL SAVINGS:

www.tiferetjournal.com/subscription-sale

ISSN 1547-2906 © 2018 SPRING/SUMMER 2018

Contents
● ● ● ●

"Thank you for this journal which combines spiritual issues, imaginative issues, esthetic issues. All of those, I think, need to be in the mix for the richly lived life, the richly observed life."

– MOLLY PEACOCK, *former President of the Poetry Society of America*

From our Editor-In-Chief

Dearest Readers,

As I write this, I am still feeling the afterglow of the Tiferet Journal reading at the Association of Writers and Writing Programs Conference in Tampa, Florida. Being in a roomful of Tiferet contributors and fans, hearing voices spring from the page into full three dimensional life, filled me with so much awe and gratitude for the ever-evolving community we are building together, a community of open-hearted seekers, fiercely committed to creative and authentic expression. I feel that same community as I hold this issue—we may not be in a physical room together, but the voices in these pages reverberate together, creating their own new and sacred space.

To echo our baffling times, this issue is full of questions—questions about identity, questions about faith, questions about what it means to be human—questions with no easy answers. And, as many of the pieces in this issue remind us, that's okay—we don't always need answers. Sometimes answers keep us from the true nature of things. Sometimes, as Siamak Vossoughi notes in his short story, "On the Hook", "wondering together (is) answer enough." How lucky we are to be able to wonder along with the writers and artists in these pages.

Whitman famously wrote "I am large. I contain multitudes" and so many of the pieces in this issue deal with multiplicity of self, with the ways we can become strangers to ourselves, the ways this can sometimes unsettle us, sometimes free us. In her essay, "How to Become a Ghost", Laraine Herring writes "You thought you were special, but you're just like everyone else, thinking your hold on yourself was unbreakable. Maybe it ultimately is, but even the stealthiest of winter animals go into hiding." And Wryly T. McCutcheon, in their poem, "Contents", writes:

"I contain undocumented senses
I contain pots boiling over
I contain the heat and homogenizing force of written history
I contain the waiting and unwritten
I contain already
 the wisdom in the lessons
 I'm learning and unlearning"

We hold so many selves inside our skin. It feels appropriate that the theme for this issue's Tiferet Tifs is "Transformation." Sometimes, as Katharine Coldiron reminds us in "Becoming as Destruction", we have to obliterate once was in order to change, just as a caterpillar has to liquefy to become a butterfly. Sometimes our only constant is change, and this can offer its own sense of liberation, as LaCoya Katoe writes in "The Women Who Love Me": "again, I make new attempts at freedom, always praying palms up, fighting the urge to clasp my fingers around anyone I might become."

In this issue, we are also delighted to feature writing from three recent guests to our podcast, Tiferet Talk—Martin Moran, Lesléa Newman, and William Kenower—along with an essay from our podcast's esteemed producer, RJ Jeffreys. You can listen to our in-depth interviews with them (and other fascinating and soulful guests) at http://tiferetjournal.com/tiferet-talk/

Thank you for being part of this vibrant Tiferet community. Let's keep wondering together.

With love and gratitude,
Gayle

Gayle Brandeis
Editor in Chief

POETRY

Cosmos

Christine Valters Paintner

That first moment,
explosion of fire and fury
a stampede of suns
light poured into the dark
chalice of space
sparks wheel across
the dome overhead.

We look to the inky sky
to track creatures formed there,
crab and scorpion, lion and bear
stars which died a million years ago
still throbbing with impossible light.

When I close my eyes
I see them still and it seems
they reach to me and I to them.

Is it gravity, or a longing kindled
by stardust within me
or the doorway to forever?

NONFICTION

Allegiances

Judith Barrington

The shallow white box arrived at my house by special delivery. I wasn't expecting anything; it wasn't my birthday and I had resisted ordering from the latest catalogues. Sometimes I receive unsolicited books for review—usually awful books with titles like *Lady Somerville and the Fencing Master*, or *How to Cook with Parsnips*—but this parcel wasn't even remotely book-shaped.

My dog, natural enemy of mail carriers, UPS employees, and FedEx people, barked herself into a frenzy, and continued long after the offending carrier had disappeared. Called away by a ringing phone, I was drawn back to the porch ten minutes later by the dog's continuing growls and arrived just in time to witness the cat spraying the corner of the package. Avoiding the damp and pungent portion, I sliced through tape and eased the lid off. White paper covered something stiff and canvassy. I ripped away the paper and there, neatly folded to the exact size of the box, lay a United States flag.

I might not immediately have recognized that it was a flag had it not been for the official-looking certificate that lay face up in the very middle of the folded material. Printed on yellowish, pseudo-parchment paper, it bore a small replica of the White House surrounded by the words, "The Architect of the Capitol, 1793." On each side of this was printed a flag, the one on the left showing a circle of thirteen stars, the one on the right bearing fifty. In case I missed the point, large blue type between them announced, "The Flag of the United States of America."

This was not the sort of thing that normally arrived on my front porch. For a moment I wondered if I had done something wrong, guilt an easy response to the unexpected, even though petty crimes— the only kind I was likely to have committed— do not usually result in the delivery of a flag. Was it there to remind me of stern justice, or my patriotic duty? Perhaps it was merely a reminder of where I was: "You're in America now. Better shape up."

As I carried the box into the house, I read the smaller typewritten message: "This is to certify that the accompanying flag was flown over the United States Capitol on April 26, 1994, at the request of the Honorable Elizabeth Furse, Member of Congress." Then, after a space, almost as an afterthought: "This flag was flown for Judith Barrington on the occasion of becoming a U.S. citizen on April 29, 1994."

Tiferet

It was true that I had recently become a U.S. citizen, but it seemed unlikely that Congress would have decided to celebrate the event. I was hardly a great catch, having always been a radical griper about America and its evil-doings in the world. Indeed, it had taken me a full eighteen years of life in the U.S. to steel myself for the nationality transition. I certainly wasn't a grateful immigrant fleeing horrible circumstances or falling to my knees onto pavements of gold.

I remained skeptical for a few hours until I learned from my friend Phyllis, who worked for Congresswoman Furse and who had been responsible for the gift, that members of Congress fly flags for all kinds of people to acknowledge their patriotic red-letter days. After the flying, some lowly person whose job it is to dispatch flags to worthy citizens, sends along the very item (or so they say) that waved in the Washington breeze to honor the recipient. My flag, however, looked, to my suspicious eye, far too pristine, with its crisp folds and absence of smuts or wrinkles, to have ascended the flagpole even on a sunny day. What did it really mean?

* * *

It hadn't been an easy decision. I started thinking about it several years after becoming a permanent resident of the U.S. and was surprised to discover that I was more attached to being British than I would have supposed. This was confusing since I distrusted nationalism and had frequently spoken out about it in the context of feminist political activities. "As American as apple pie" had been the banner under which we campaigned for something in the late seventies (was it reproductive freedom or comparable worth?) and I had fought against the slogan, having just read Winifred Holtby's stern book on nationalism. We should convince people that justice is important for its own sake, I had claimed—not appeal to their knee-jerk chauvinism, or their sweet tooth. It's that same unthinking emotion, stirred up by the inflammatory word "patriotism," which, I declared, leads to all kinds of injustice and to wars. No, we should not encourage it, nor should we manipulate it for our own ends. But I hadn't reckoned on the power of the apple pie, even over radical feminists. The slogan stayed.

If I was so opposed to nationalism then, how could my own nationality really matter? I couldn't explain it satisfactorily, even to myself. All I knew was that it had something to do with identity—that my Britishness, in spite of the fact that barely a trace of English accent remained, was a part of how I saw myself. Without it, I would be less attached to my place in the world. Less myself.

I know that some people don't have to be attached geographically in order to identify with a community: historically, the Jews are a great example of a people who looked to the group, and not the ground it lived on, for that sense of belonging.

But my own heritage was very different. I did feel identified with the soil of England. Never without a place to call their own, my ancestors had been rooted for generations in places I knew intimately. I had walked through Banstead churchyard where my mother's Lambert ancestors lay beneath mild English grass, under old beech and oak trees, their names engraved on tilting, moss-covered gravestones that go back hundreds of years. I understood my parents' allegiance to the British colony during the years they lived in Barcelona. I had noticed, too, that every single expatriate Briton I knew still referred to the old country as "home," sometimes after living abroad for thirty or forty years and becoming a citizen of another country. When they would ask me about my next trip "home," I refused to collude with this reference, saying lightly, "My home is here now," but they would look at me oddly. I was a bit of a traitor, they seemed to imply, even after all this time.

In spite of Britain's drastic decline in world influence, a majority of its white people can still barely conceal how fortunate they consider themselves not to have been born French or American, to say nothing of non-Western. Not only do many of them feel this way, but a good percentage are willing to say so out loud in front of anyone from another country. Not long ago, the "Brexit" referendum revealed the deep pockets of this xenophobia that lingers even today. I dare say quite a lot of other national groups feel like this too, but few seem to consider themselves as entitled to the sentiment as the British.

During my years in the U.S., American culture has enjoyed peaks of popularity in Europe, but still, when I return to Britain, I find remnants of the old anti-Americanism that was rampant when I was a child, particularly among the older generations. My parents were fairly typical of middle class people in the fifties and sixties: they considered Americans to be loud, ostentatious, and rude. When we went on holiday to Spain, we would often find American military families, who were stationed in Germany, vacationing with us at our hotel. According to my parents, their cars were unnecessarily long with an excess of chrome that my father considered flashy; their children ran wild around the dining room, and, according to my mother, had no manners whatsoever; and, as both my parents agreed, the adults talked about money in an unbelievably vulgar way. When my sister spent two years in New York during her early married life, she returned full of enthusiasm for things American. Her expanded horizons, however, were universally ignored by my family. They considered her sadly misguided.

By the time I considered becoming an American, I had shaken off most of these attitudes. I was a politically active member of my new U.S. community, yet I was completely disenfranchised, allowed to vote in neither American nor British elections. I was also somewhat vulnerable as a non-citizen, even with the status of permanent resident. If something dreadful happened politically which I felt obliged to protest in public, I might be arrested. If that happened, I could be deported, losing the whole life I had built up. The thought of being forced out of my community made me realize just how rooted I had become.

Over the years, what I had missed most about England was the land itself: the smells of grass and sea; the silhouette of the downs I had grown up walking and riding across, the particularity of moorland, bog, beechwood, and rolling farmland ploughed and planted for centuries. My attachment to the primroses and the cuckoos of an English spring, to the patterns of tile and brick on Sussex cottages, and to the proportions of country lanes with dense hedges that barely skimmed both sides of my car, remained stronger than my attachment to British people as a group, or even to styles of conversation or other cultural habits that I had found difficult to let go of, so firmly entrenched had they been.

This love of the land was a sensual thing that embraced farmyard smells, the shape of kissing-gates, and the patterns of shadows racing across sheep-shorn hills. It was in my body, and no amount of rational argument could change it. And, in fact, it didn't ever change—not even when I started to form emotional and visceral attachments to New World landscapes. It turned out to be a matter not of replacement but of expansion: I simply found in myself the capacity to love more and different geographies. This same body that responded to a Welsh dry-stone wall, started to respond also to the smells of rainforests and sagebrush deserts; my eye became accustomed to the proportions of canyons and mile-wide rivers.

More than elections or politics, more than seats on government panels or eligibility for U.S. fellowships, more, even, than safety from deportation, it was this cautious involvement with a new landscape, this slow, vulnerable putting down of roots into the soil, that ultimately made changing my citizenship seem the right thing to do.

* * *

The naturalization ceremony was held in the Bonneville Power Administration auditorium. We about-to-be-new citizens were seated in the center portion of the hall, over a hundred of us. Visitors sat in the side sections, some poised with video cameras to record the moment when their newly-arrived family members would receive their certificates, stamped with a gold seal, admitting them to membership of one of the most sought-after clubs in the world. As we filed into our seats, volunteers at the end of each row handed out small U.S. flags, which we held on our laps as we sat, eyeing one another. Then the volunteers hooked ropes across the ends of the aisles and stood guard by the exit doors as if we might all suddenly think better of the whole thing and make a dash for it.

I was sitting between a man who looked Vietnamese and a young woman from Central America, possibly Mexico. Looking around, I saw that I was one of a tiny minority of Caucasians. It dawned on me, as I studied the faces surrounding me, that for many people in the room it was a momentous occasion—perhaps the pinnacle of years of working towards this moment. Even if they had already dealt with the disillusionment or shock of a first encounter with American racism, some of them were experiencing this day as a salvation from hunger, war, or poverty, an escape from brutal, day-to-day tyranny, a chance at the thing we call liberty. As a woman, I've experienced discrimination and, as a lesbian I've struggled against the pernicious effects of homophobia, which I would never minimize in the range of human sufferings. Throughout my lifetime, Britain and America have both been rampant with the prejudices that impinge on my personal well-being, yet I differed from most of these newcomers in that I could hardly look at the United States as a refuge from these forms of injustice.

An Immigration official came to the podium and asked us all to stand. Some of us rose to our feet immediately while others, who had not understood, had to be nudged or gestured into standing. Still clutching our flags, we looked towards the platform, a sea of dark heads—Southeast Asian, South American, Central American, Arabic, and African—out of which rose three tall, fair ones, all at least a foot taller than the rest. These heads and shoulders seemed to sprout as the shoots of lilies sprout from the dark leaves that lie flat and dense across a pond. English, German, and Swiss, we were three Europeans in a world that had, up to now, always allowed us to believe that we stood close to its center. But not here. In this room, I glimpsed with exhilaration the rightness of the great experiment—the ideal of true equality—that, however flawed in practice, is the registered goal of the United States of America.

Raising our right hands, we recited a long oath, none of which I now remember except the part about renouncing "foreign princes and potentates," which made me want to laugh. Then we sat down to listen to another Immigration official tell us about our new country. He started with the glories of the physical geography: mountains, rivers, forests; the wheatfields of the midwest and the great cities. I had no quarrel with this: it seemed entirely appropriate since we were pledging our allegiance not just to a vast society, but also to a particular piece of the earth. Then he told us that America was a country made great by immigrants, which was also a nice idea as long as you didn't happen to be Native American, and he threw out the names of many people who had come here from other parts of the world to play an important role in the country's development—every single one of them a white man. Then, his voice swelling with emotion, he declared, "This is a Christian country built on Christian values."

I don't know what he said after that. I looked across the hall to where my Jewish partner and my friends were sitting. They looked my way and raised their eyebrows, shrugging their shoulders in disbelief. Then I looked around my section and wondered how many of the new immigrants consider themselves Christians. I tuned back into the speech, just as Mr. Immigration was working himself up to a weary kind of climax. Waving his skinny arms, he spoke of justice and the vision of the early settlers. Then he dropped his final bombshell: what America is all about, he said, is "Life, liberty, and the pursuit of property."

For a minute, I didn't catch it, though it didn't sound right. Nobody else seemed to notice as the word "property" clicked into my mind. I looked across the room again at my friends, who were laughing out loud. *Property?* we mouthed at each other.

As soon as the speech ended, we stepped up one at a time to receive our certificates, some accompanied by the popping flashbulbs of family members' cameras. Then the officials disappeared and the ceremony wound down with a performance by the children of the Harriet Tubman Elementary School—by far the most lively and inspiring part of the program. Lined up in their best clothes (one obviously wearing her mother's hat), twenty-five second graders faced the audience while another three or four faced the back of the stage as they sang a selection of songs, accompanied by Mrs. Weaver at the piano. "America the Beautiful" was delivered with gusto, though not always on key, and "The Star Spangled Banner" made several of my near neighbors cry. Then, as the children ran down the steps from the stage, the ropes at the end of the aisles were unhooked, and all of us new Americans, little flags and certificates in our hands, surged out to mingle with our compatriots.

"Christian country indeed!" exclaimed my group all the way through the lobby and down the street. By the time we reached home, we had hatched a plan. First we called the Jewish Federation; then Congresswoman Furse. A few weeks later, we heard that the welcome speech had been modified. The Christians and property were out; happiness was back in. But I don't know about that list of famous immigrants. Are there any people of color or women on it yet, I wonder?

* * *

We gave a party to celebrate my new status. All the friends who had helped at different times through different stages of my journey to U.S. citizenship gathered. There was champagne and beer; laughter and reminiscence. A large, chocolate cake, ordered specially for the occasion, was decorated with the words of that staunch anti-nationalist, Virginia Woolf: "As a woman, I have no country. As a woman, my country is the whole world." On each side of the cake, in the middle of the dining table, was a small flag in a stand: on the left, a British Union Jack; on the right, the Stars and Stripes. My plan was to burn both during the course of the evening. "Citizen of the world" had a nice ring to it. An end to flag-waving!

Long before I moved to the U.S., I had begun to question nationalism, even though certain things persisted in triggering my emotions—not flags, but songs such as "Jerusalem" with its words by William Blake ("England's green and pleasant land" and "those dark satanic mills"), as well as some of the historic buildings at the heart of British history such as Canterbury Cathedral. Pageantry involving carriages and royal waves from balconies left me cold, whereas brass bands playing the national anthem at the Olympics managed to push an emotional button every time. Even when I recognized my susceptibility, I couldn't entirely eradicate it; its grip was as tenacious as the grip of wedding marches and orange blossom, which used to make me teary despite being legally excluded from the ritual.

As a newcomer to the U.S., I was able not only to get more perspective on British patriotic symbols, but also to perceive the emptiness of the American ones— the flag in particular. Flags, of course, figure in the activities of most nations. The first act of the mountaineering hero at the summit is to plant a flag. This is his or her way of saying, "I do this for the glory of my country." It says, "I stake out this high spot on the earth as belonging to my people." It says, "You may think this is a fun hike with friendly competition between individuals, but it's also a deadly serious contest between nations."

There may be no danger in countries competing with one another for glory in the sporting arena but there is certainly immense harm in using the power of the flag to lure young people towards a reckless death in war. The piece of canvas, starred and striped in red, white, and blue, is a highly effective short-cut around thoughtful decision-making; a cheap way to make very complex things seem far too simple.

When I worked in schools as a visiting artist, if I was scheduled for first period, I tried to arrive in the classroom a few minutes late so I wouldn't have to discuss why I didn't pledge allegiance to the flag. If I was caught out and had to explain myself, I told the children how much I love the ideals on which our country is built and that I love, too, the land itself. I told them that for me the flag is a shallow symbol that gets in the way of remembering what it really stands for. It's better, I would suggest, when saying the pledge, to think not about some grand word like "freedom" but about some real place in their country that they loved, whether it was the park where they played or the beach they visited on a vacation. Picture something you can see and smell and touch, I said. Something that has colors and sounds. Something you could draw a picture of or make up a song about.

It had seemed a good idea to burn the two flags at my party, but I should have known they would let me down. When the moment came the two pieces of red, white and blue material, liberally sprinkled with lighter fluid, refused to blaze up in a statement of triumphant rejection. Instead, being made of cheap polyester, they produced acrid, black smoke, and shriveled into little globs of melted plastic. The smell was terrible.

* * *

That night we celebrated my choice to become an American—or to be more precise, a citizen of the United States. To this day I have a hard time identifying with "immigrant," a name that makes me feel as if I should be standing in a long overcoat next to a battered brown suitcase somewhere cold, thinking about how to simplify my name. I mean no disrespect in using this stereotyped image of those who came here during the early years of the twentieth century—in fact they will probably always remain for me the real immigrants: the adventurous ones who took a chance, and the lucky ones who escaped with their lives. Still, different as I am from them, I have come to share with many of them an important feeling about our adopted country.

It's easy to be cynical about the shortcomings of America; much harder to admit to feelings that might seem naive. I have come to love the grand ideals that lie beneath all that is obviously wrong with the United States—those ideals that I glimpsed for a moment at my naturalization ceremony —the multiracial childrens' choir—a bunch of kids, some full of hope, some bored or hungry, and others proudly singing their hearts out to welcome more than a hundred of us into their home. And while I know that not all those kids have an equal chance at succeeding in lives they aspire to, I also know that underneath the prejudice they will likely have to face, is a solid ideal—even if we citizens do not yet know how to make it a living reality.

To me, Old Glory will always be just a piece of canvas in a white box like the one they say flew over the White House in my honor. I don't know what I will do with it: burn it or fly it from the roof or wrap it around my body for a piece of performance art? Whatever I do, I'm pretty sure I'll keep it, especially since I now realize one very significant fact about it—a fact that reflects the profound ambivalence I once felt about taking the leap into citizenship. On the day my flag flew above the White House to celebrate my naturalization, Richard Nixon had just died. All the flags flew at half-mast. .

POETRY

On The Day My Father Died: Hungarian Refugees Bring Food

Edwin Romond

Above the voices of grief in our kitchen
I heard a knock at our front door
and found Hungarian refugee neighbors
with my buddy, Tibor, who already knew
some English. They were crying
as they stood with bowls of *gulyas*
and pastry trays of *orahnjaca*.
They whispered, "*sajnalom, sajnalom*"
and Tibor said, "We are sorry

about your father." Mrs. Tackash
repeated over and over, "*jo ember*"
and Tibor told me, "She says your father
was a good man." My mother invited
them in to join our other neighbors
but they just wanted to give us dishes
and plates still warm beneath waxed paper
filled with their savory and sweet
gifts of friendship and condolence

from the homeland they were forced to flee.
They all hugged my mother and me then
stepped down from our porch and
looked like angels beneath the gold
of Albert St. streetlights. Mrs. Hegedus
called up from the sidewalk, "*Istenaldjon*"
and Tibor said, "It means, "'God bless you'"
and I did my best to answer, "*Istenaldjon*,"
a Hungarian prayer in our American night.

NONFICTION

Mrs. Burry

Teri Fuller

Who discovered the other first in the restaurant on Easter Sunday, Mrs. Burry did not know. But there they found themselves: she and the little girl. Even though she had never had any of her own, Mrs. Burry's world was constructed of children. They served as living walls and doors to her world, a framework for her daily existence. Mrs. Burry watched them run down the aisles of the grocery store, pump their legs hard and high on swing sets, and run through her yard late at night, playing Ghost in the Graveyard.

The outside of Mrs. Burry's house, orchestrated by Mr. Burry, was well-manicured. A brick-paved driveway was lined on both sides with a hedge of rose bushes, all deep red. A matching brick-paved walkway to the covered porch ran all the way around the two-story, brick house which had two white columns running down the front. "Stately," others said. And there were rocking chairs, Mrs. Burry's only insistence, each a different color, spread evenly across the porch. They were arranged according to the colors of the rainbow: red, orange, yellow, green, blue, indigo, and violet.

The inside of Mrs. Burry's stately house, however, was *not* stately at all. The first floor hinted at the second: a makeshift hospital for one. The kitchen counters were full of prescription bottles, some empty, some full and unused. A medicine chart she never followed on the fridge. Names of emergency contacts she never called next to that. The curtains were drawn on both levels of the house, and it felt perpetually like sunset; the sun going away soon. On the couch, a pile of messy blankets. Mrs. Burry liked to watch reruns of *The Golden Girls*. She knew she was Dorothy, but she wanted to be Blanche.

Upstairs smelled of chlorine. Mrs. Burry poured it into the toilet each time she got sick from the chemotherapy drugs. Vomiting was for the second floor, she thought, so she held it in until she could make it to the master bathroom. Knees. Bald head in the center of the bowl. Vomit. Wipe mouth with towel on sink. Vomit a second time. Wipe again. Spit. Flush. Flush again. Then pour in the bleach, which she let sit until the next time she used the toilet. In her bedroom, she had leaned her regular mattress up against the wall and had a hospital bed delivered. One that could go up, down, and even raise up to knee level. It helped her in and out out of bed, but without a smile or a friendly word. It had railings she hadn't used yet, but that the medical supply company assured her she'd be glad she had bought one day.

She lined the top of her oak wood dresser with newspaper, and more medicine bottles sat on top, one red-capped bottle of pain pills and one blue-capped bottle of sleeping pills. There was also a gallon of expensive spring water from the store, one of her few indulgences. Several glasses rested on the newspaper, too, and she often wondered which glass was the cleanest. White sheets had come with the hospital bed, but she had not washed them once since getting them—even though they smelled of sweat and were no longer taut and smooth. And her one cat, Dora, spent most of her time in the corner of her room where the litter box was. Mrs. Burry was accustomed to the smell of used kitty litter and only changed it when the box began to overflow.

At night, when Mrs. Burry was in bed, Dora would jump softly onto the hospital bed, circle three times next to Mrs. Burry's right hip, and burrow in beside her. "You're a good kitty," Mrs. Burry would say. Then she would stroke the cat's thick black fur while pellets of kitty litter fell out and onto the bed.

Mrs. Burry married only once. A salesman. He was handsome, and they slept together on their first date. He said it was love at first sight, and she believed him. That was fifty-two years ago, and now Mrs. Burry was seventy-two. Mr. Burry bought their current house two years before he ran off with that other woman. That was six months ago. She always said "that other woman" instead of "my sister." When people in town asked about him, she said that Mr. Burry was traveling, even though most people knew what happened.

Mrs. Burry tried to convince herself that Mr. Burry would be back. That he still loved her and not her sister. That when he came back, she would get rid of the hospital bed and put her regular mattress back on its frame and put on fresh sheets. She would grow her hair long for him and stop vomiting. She would have reconstruction surgery and have breasts bigger than she had before. Perky like the night of their first date.

After Mr. Burry left, Mrs. Burry did not put pictures of him away. In fact, she went to the unfinished basement, rarely visited, and unpacked more. Ones she had forgotten. One of Mr. Burry in his early twenties, the decade he fell in love with her at first sight. One of Mr. and Mrs. Burry when they took a cruise from Miami to the Bahamas for their twenty-fifth wedding anniversary, in 1992. Mr. Burry in a short-sleeve dress shirt with a coordinated tie and she with a dress adorned with tropical flowers, up against the cruise ship's rail. Mrs. Burry set down the picture and looked at her chest. "Is that what my breasts looked like?" she said. She had been a C-cup; she liked her breasts. She knew Mr. Burry had liked them, too. Then she felt her cold, smooth, beach-ball head. "Was that my hair?" she said, studying the long, curly black tendrils that showered down upon her dress. That was only one of two vacations they took over the past fifty-two years. The other was to Washington D.C. in 2000. To the Smithsonian. It was part of Mr. Burry's sales territory. "You must see the Smithsonian," Mr. Burry had told her. He had gone without her several times before, but when they went together, she was surprised. She thought the Smithsonian was one museum, not a collection of them. They were happy that week. They looked at portraits of the presidents, read about the largest squid ever discovered, and saw spaceships that had really gone to space. Her favorite, though, was the Postal Museum. They studied the gallery of stamps, and Mr. Burry said, "They should put your face on a stamp." Mrs. Burry bet he had never said that to anyone else before, and she turned her face to the right, showing it to him in profile.

The incident with the little girl on Easter Sunday happened at Preservation, a nearby French bistro. Mrs. Burry's cousin and her cousin's husband, contacts on her fridge she never called, invited her to join them for brunch. Mrs. Burry's cousin and her cousin's husband lived just one town over: a twenty-minute drive, and the restaurant was only five minutes from Mrs. Burry's house. Mrs. Burry wanted to say no and stay home. Her last chemotherapy treatment was just one week prior, and she was still weak. She was no longer throwing up each day, but she had no appetite. And the tingling in her hands and feet had gotten worse in the past month. Mrs. Burry's oncologist gave her medication to help with what the doctor called "peripheral neuropathy," but it only made her even more nauseous. She preferred the tingling, the pain, and the numbness to that.

The day before Easter, Mrs. Burry went to her closet. She usually rotated between two pairs of sweatpants with matching sweatshirts that she bought at Walmart. They were furry on the inside, and when the material moved, it petted her lonely skin. One set was gray. The other dark gray. There were also clothes from before her diagnosis in the closet. Before Mr. Burry ran away with the other woman. There were all shades of colors, like the chairs that sat on her wrap-around porch. As she filed through the clothes, she stopped on one long, lace dress. It was violet. She closed her eyes and imagined someone squeezing and molding thousands of violets to make that dress. Just for her. Mr. Burry never liked it. "Too flashy," he said. She didn't wear it after that, after Mr. Burry's niece's wedding back in 1997, but she kept it in her closet anyway. She liked the low neckline. How it had showed off her C-cup breasts—before cancer. The slit up the back that hinted at her panties beneath. She liked the long sleeves that flared out like rays from the sun. And she even had matching violet satin pumps. She had taken her tailor a swatch from the dress, a small patch cut from the bottom hem, and had the shoes dyed the same color.

She knew she shouldn't wear that dress to brunch with her cousin and her cousin's husband, so she found something more sensible, something Mr. Burry would have approved of. A long, delicate floral print dress with a high neckline. She would need help zipping it up in back, but her cousin would surely help when they picked her up. She got on her knees and looked at her shoes. She saw the violet pumps and moved her shaking, tingling fingers towards them until her fingers hurt too much. Then, she sat back on her legs, breathed in and out slowly to steady herself, and eyed a pair of tan flats. She had bought them because they were sensible.

Downstairs, Mrs. Burry walked in her dark grey sweatsuit to the counter. She moved the pill bottles around. She set ones she did not need to the left and ones she did need to the right. With little painful gasps, she pressed down and twisted off the caps and shook out the pills. She liked the way they looked on the counter. The different colors. Shapes. Numbers and letters. "This is quite enough to fill me up," she said, dismissing the idea of breakfast. The pills were all hers. All meant to make her better, and she could *always* count on the pills being there.

The night before Easter, Mrs. Burry was nervous. It certainly would be rude not to take anything from the brunch buffet, and she did not wish to insult her cousin and her cousin's husband. There would be scrambled eggs, crisp bacon, sausage, and waffles and crepes prepared on site. These things would have thrilled Mrs. Burry before the diagnosis, but now even the thought of them made her ill.

Mrs. Burry climbed the steps to her bedroom. The other two rooms were closed off. One was Mr. Burry's office, and the other was a guest bedroom no one ever stayed in. She passed two closed doors before making it to the end of the hall. Now was her favorite part of the day. When she took her sleeping pill. Mrs. Burry didn't take sleeping medication before the diagnosis. She had occasional restless nights but nothing like what happened after cancer. She stayed up all night. Got out of bed. Sometimes had a bowl of cereal and then lay on the couch. Sometimes the sun would come up, and she would not have slept at all. But now Mrs. Burry had Alisomb. Her oncologist said it wasn't addictive. That it was safe. And every night, she looked forward to it like a rich dessert at the end of a meal. The directions were to take the pill and immediately lie down in bed. She learned, however, that she could take the pill, not lie down, and experience its hypnotic effects. Go to a new world. One where Mr. Burry had not run away with that other woman. One where she still had her C-cup breasts. One where the inside of her house, decorated by an interior designer Mr. Burry had hired, was still as stately as the outside.

Mrs. Burry grabbed the closest, fullest water glass and swallowed the Alisomb. She even liked the pungent aftertaste that hinted at approaching relief.

Tiferet

Instead of getting into bed like she should, Mrs. Burry walked to her dark maple desk, which was four skinny legs holding up one long plank of wood. Upon the desk were pictures of Mr. Burry. Some just of him. Some with them both. She stared at the photographs as she felt the drug kicking in. The day's anxieties over what to wear and what to eat tomorrow melted away, dripped out of her brain through her ears and down her skin like hot wax. "Mr. Burry," she said softly, "You are still here. With me."

During the day, after the sleeping pill wore off, Mrs. Burry wasn't sure that God existed, but when she had taken her sleeping pill, she was. She could feel something spiritual around her. In her. Even in inanimate things like the photographs of Mr. Burry. Even the chair. She put her hands on the arms of the chair and glided them up and down the polished maple wood. "Am I too heavy for you? Shall I get off?" she asked it.

The chair didn't mind, so she stayed. She looked and touched and felt God until she couldn't keep her eyes open any more. She made it to her bed, where Dora soon followed, and went to sleep.

God left sometime in the night, and on Easter morning, it was only Mrs. Burry and Dora. The pain was worse than usual. Deep in her bones. Where the cancer had spread. Mrs. Burry groggily pressed a button that raised the head of the hospital bed, reached over to her nightstand, took a bottle, pressed down with a guttural moan, and twisted.

"Oh," she cried in pain, and fell back, defeated.

She wouldn't have made such a noise if Mr. Burry were there, but he was gone, and she could let the raw, uncensored noises of her body out.

She tried again. Bottle. Cap. Press. Twist.

"Finally!" Mrs. Burry exclaimed, though she did not realize it was the blue-capped bottle and not the red that she opened.

One wouldn't do. Two pain pills. Her hand trembled as she shook two pills into the palm of her right hand. Like a catapult, her hand shot up and thrust the pills into her mouth, seized a glass of water, and she swallowed the medicine.

She relaxed, closed her eyes, and summoned the numbness to follow.

After minutes or perhaps an hour, she did not know, she raised the back of the bed even more, pivoted her legs to the left side, and stood.

The pain had not gone away, but the pain no longer mattered.

She focused instead on the creamy carpet under her feet like whipped frosting and stepped delightedly to the master bathroom, savoring every fiber of the carpet Mr. Burry had picked out. Her toenails were long, and her two big toenails were thick and yellow with fungus, and she burrowed them down into the white threads.

When she reached the frame of the bathroom door, she stopped. She felt young and old, all at the same time. She raised her hands and fixed them on either side of the door's frame. Just like when she was a girl. When she would shimmy her way up with her little body. Hands and feet wriggling to the top. A child's victory over gravity. She breathed in the airy memory.

Then, one foot on the cold, carefully laid tile in the bathroom that hadn't been cleaned since Mr. Burry left. The grout now dark gray instead of bright white. Usually the cold alarmed her in the morning, but today it felt exhilarating—like jumping into a cold pool on a hot summer's day. She was excited by it. She skated across it, the soles of her feet swooshing against the glassy plane.

For a moment, she had forgotten why she had come to the bathroom. Then she remembered. It was Easter, and she was having brunch with her cousin and her cousin's husband.

"Brush teeth. Pills. Get dressed. Find my purse," she said. She talked out loud to herself often, even more now that she was alone.

Forgetting to brush her teeth, she returned to the bedroom, where she unthinkingly opened the curtains on both windows. Light shone on what had been dark for so long, and Mrs. Burry smiled.

"Was it my morning pills I was supposed to get next?" she asked herself. "Yes," she answered, and walked downstairs. She studied the medicine bottles on the counter.

Was it the bottles on the left she needed to take, or the ones on the right? she wondered.

She bent down to investigate. To the left. Then to the right.

"Such formal names," she said, chuckling. Tamoxifen. Herceptin. Methylprednisolone.

She heard a neighbor's dog bark and remembered it was the pills on the right.

One by one, she opened each bottle. Bottle. Cap. Press. Twist. One pill from each. She lined them up in front of her on the counter. The marble countertop that Mr. Burry had chosen. The countertop Mrs. Burry thought was too expensive. Six total. The spectrum of sizes and colors mesmerized her. She touched each one, placing them in a straight horizontal line from biggest to smallest. Two were approximately the same size, so she decided to sort those two by color. Darker one first and then lighter. With her right index finger, she traced an oval around the array. She had not understood the grace of the milky, marble stone before. How solid. Sturdy. She placed both of her hands on each side of the pills and leaned into the counter. The counter didn't move. She could not push it down. Its touch told her of its history. It whispered to her about the mining. Raw, colossal slabs harvested from the sides of mountains. Maybe I'm from Italy, the marble said. An aged, contemplative voice.

Mr. Burry had been to Italy. "There's marble everywhere," he had told her. "Even the curbs on the streets are made of it." Mrs. Burry thought he was the luckiest man alive to have seen marble curbs.

She could feel Italy with all its marble within her. She shut her eyes and saw the Italian mountains from a plane. High above the Alps. Then a revelation. The white on top was not snow but marble, and she stood still in that moment of awe.

She came down from the plane, the mountains with marble, to the pills.

"Water," she said, grabbing a glass.

"One, two, three, four, five, six."

From left to right: a big, maroon oval with the number six hundred in black, a leaner ivory oval with unreadable numbers printed on both ends, an even smaller oval green on one end and ivory on the other, a plump, shiny maroon egg of a pill with no writing at all, half of a white pill—jagged where it had been split from its other half—and her favorite, the smallest, a flat oval cerulean pill.

In succession, she took them: biggest to smallest. Her tongue caressed each one, letting the ones without a gelatin coating dissolve slightly before swallowing.

Mr. Burry had been an exact man, and he would not have permitted Mrs. Burry to take her pills in that manner. He would have bought her a pill dispenser. One with a vacancy for each day of the week. He would have demanded she put away the bottles in the cabinet where the rest of the medicine went. Next to his over-the-counter medicine, his Advil, Pepcid, and Tums, which he rarely took. He wasn't one to take much medicine.

He would have made sure she was dressed hours before Mrs. Burry's cousin and her cousin's husband came to pick her up for Easter brunch. But Mr. Burry wasn't there, and for the first time, Mrs. Burry was glad. She was glad he wasn't there with his pressed suits, which he had tailored as he lost weight over the years—convinced that an aging man should become thinner, not thicker. His body thinning along with his hair. His still-youthful face.

Instead of getting dressed, she said, "Just one episode," and with a dry mouth, walked to the couch. Mr. Burry had wanted the black leather couch. She routinely found it cold and unwelcoming to her skin, but as she fell gently on her side into its padding, she instead found it soothing. She burrowed her right cheek into the supple leather and closed her eyes, relishing in its comfort. She had gone to the couch to watch *The Golden Girls*, but the couch seduced her, and she wanted to feel the couch against more than just her cheek.

She slid her hands down and wiggled her pajama bottoms off. Then her white, large panties. Then her pajama top. It her nakedness, she felt the essence of the dusty leather.

"It was never supposed to warm me. I was supposed to warm it," she realized.

She turned. To her stomach. Her other side. To her back. She buried her bald head deep into the downy seat of the couch and rolled it from side to side.

"Every part of me," she said, promising the couch she would share all of herself.

The couch did not whisper to her like the marble, but it felt satisfied. Mrs. Burry smiled at its contentment, forgetting all about her show, serenely falling back to sleep.

When she woke, she looked at the clock above the television. A clock Mr. Burry had bought at the overpriced furniture store in town. Big Roman numerals. It barked at her: 11:45am.

Mrs. Burry's cousin and her cousin's husband would be there in 15 minutes.

It was hard for Mrs. Burry to rouse from the couch, but she willed herself.

Upstairs, she put her right hand on the sensible floral dress, but pain bulleted through her fingers. Then she understood what she had done. She had taken the Alisomb, not the Norcom.

"Just need pain pills," she said, and she returned to her nightstand covered in newspapers, squatted down to read the titles on the bottles, and found it.

"N-O-R-C-O-M. Norcom. This is the one."

Bottle. Cap. Press. Twist. Two more pills catapulted into her mouth, and she swallowed.

And rather than dreading brunch with her cousin and her cousin's husband, she was most excited. A forgotten feeling since Mr. Burry had left.

Again, she forgot what she had been doing. She struggled to think.

"My dress," she realized, and walked into the bathroom.

"No, it's in the closet." She ambled back into the bedroom.

She saw the floral dress, but she could not touch it. Her eyes moved to the violet lace one. She lifted it out of the closet. She set it on the bed and went back for the shoes. Down on her knees, she slid out the dyed, matching satin pumps. With less pain in her fingers, she got up and sat them next to the dress.

Easter, she thought, is the perfect day for violets. A first sign of life. Spring.

Tiferet

Mrs. Burry had wanted to plant humble sweet violets in their yard, but Mr. Burry wanted roses.

"They're more American," he said. "Grander. They make a statement."

Mrs. Burry remembered smelling sweet violets as a child. Hunkered down in the woods behind her house, she swept the leaves aside that hid the fragrant flowers underneath. Smelling a violet isn't as easy as smelling a rose. A rose you can smell inches from your nose. Maybe even further. A violet, on the other hand, is trickier. Mrs. Burry got down on all fours and buried her nose in the fragile flowers.

She now smelled the same childhood violets in her dress.

"Why had I not smelled you before?" she asked. "I will wear you today. I'm sorry it's been so long."

Already naked, she unzipped the back of the dress and stepped in. Left foot. Then right. She steadied herself by placing her hand on the bed. She pulled the dress up. It kissed her shins, hips, stomach, bottom, chest, and arms. She wanted to perfume herself with its scent, so she bent over, running her hands up the side of her legs, her hips, and up to her chest—where her C-cup breasts used to be. Where her nipples used to be.

"I'll give them back to you," the dress told her, as if telepathically.

She fixed her hands on her chest, and she breathed in as the material on her chest pushed out from the force of her newly formed breasts.

Mrs. Burry could not reach behind her back to zip up the dress, but her cousin was an agreeable woman. Her cousin would surely help.

Then the doorbell rang as if it knew to summon help.

"Shoes first!" Mrs. Burry blurted out, placing them both on the ground, stepping in one, then the other.

Mrs. Burry was unsteady on the stairs going down, but she delighted in the smoothness of the railing under the palm of her hand. What made it so smooth? Man? Machine?

Mrs. Burry was smiling when she opened the door.

"Oh, Birdie," she said. "You are right on time."

Mrs. Burry did not notice the rattled look on her guests' faces.

Before inviting them in, she said, "Birdie, please zip me up, will you? I just couldn't get it," and Mrs. Burry turned around.

Her cousin's husband, Bill, said, "Let's go inside first, shall we?"

Mrs. Burry said, "Yes, of course. You're right. Come on in."

Mrs. Burry shut the door after them and turned again to her cousin. Mrs. Burry momentarily forgot that she was bald, and she went to lift her formerly long, graying black hair from her back and shoulders while her cousin zipped her up.

Mrs. Burry pushed out her chest and stood tall as she turned to see them. Her ankle gave out, and she started to fall to the right. Bill reached out to steady her.

Seemingly out of nowhere, Mrs. Burry asked, "Would you like to try the couch?"

Birdie and Bill did not answer but followed Mrs. Burry towards the living room—past the pills, the water glasses, the un-vacuumed floors, the heap of dirty dishes in the sink, and the garbage bags lined up against the wall adjacent to the kitchen.

Birdie said. "Is that what you're wearing to brunch?"

"Yes. Violets. I'm wearing thousands of them. Don't they smell remarkable?"

Birdie looked at her husband.

"I'm silly, aren't I? No time for the couch now," Mrs. Burry said. "It's time to eat." She was hungry, which she hadn't been in some time, and Mrs. Burry went back to the front door. Out she went with Birdie and Bill following her.

They were sure Mrs. Burry would fall down the steps, but she didn't. She stepped softly down upon the stately brick walkway in her matching satin pumps and let herself into the back seat of Bill's car.

Before Birdie and Bill got in the front, Mrs. Burry called out, "My purse! One minute. I'll be back. You stay here. I'll grab it real quick."

Inside the house again, Mrs. Burry darted up the stairs. She hadn't had the energy nor could she stand the pain from moving that quickly on the stairs for many months. But now the pain was gone, and in its place was a communion with her surroundings. In her room, she returned to the closet and looked at the collection of purses that sat on the top shelf.

"It's in the back. I'm sure of it."

She pulled down the purses with big, sudden sweeps of her arms until at last the violet beaded purse fell from above.

She hadn't thought of what to put in it. She turned to the nightstand.

She put one bottle of Alisomb and one bottle of Norcom into the purse, her paraphernalia of sickness.

"Maybe we should stay here," she heard Birdie call from downstairs. Mrs. Burry walked to the top of the stairs.

"Don't be silly, Birdie. I'm all ready. See, I've found my purse." She waved it high, without pain, above her head.

On the drive to the restaurant, Mrs. Burry fingered the tan upholstery. She liked the bumpy texture, which seemed to coordinate with each bump in the road. Neither Birdie nor Bill spoke.

Tiferet

The car sailed down the street, around corners, following Bill's commands. An obedient car, Mrs. Burry thought.

"Why don't you drop us off at the door, Bill, and you can park?" Birdie said.

"No, no need. I feel great!" Mrs. Burry said, her mind spiraling with capability.

Mrs. Burry felt beautiful—no, stunning—as she walked into the crowded restaurant. It was a festive day. Men in suits. Women in dresses. And all the children.

And the smells coming from the buffet were intoxicating. Mrs. Burry wanted it all. The eggs, the bacon, the waffles, the crepes.

"I am so glad you invited me," she told Birdie and Bill, who remained silent.

The cute, young hostess with long, straight black hair told them it would be a few minutes before their table was ready.

"Do you mind if I use the little girl's room?" Mrs. Burry asked coyly.

"Of course. Let me go with you," Birdie said.

"No need. I'll be right back. You just stay there with your handsome husband."

She had been to that restaurant once before, on one of her anniversaries with Mr. Burry. It had been a lovely evening. She remembered the bathroom was to the right in the back.

Mrs. Burry pushed at the door. She leaned in hard. It wouldn't move. Mrs. Burry backed up, looked up to make sure she was in the right place. She was. When she looked back down, she saw a sign on the door that read "Pull." She caressed the long silver bar handle and pulled hard, almost falling backwards with the motion of the door.

It was bright inside, the bulbs a sprawling, artificial sun that hurt her eyes. She stood in the entryway until someone else pulled the door open.

"Excuse me," the other woman said. She was a younger woman. In her forties. Probably a mother, Mrs. Burry thought. Mrs. Burry had never been a mother.

Mrs. Burry looked at the woman and stepped aside. The other woman with the averting eyes looked down as adults often did. Adults, Mrs. Burry learned, didn't like to see bald women. A symbol of disease, not life. Normally, this would have saddened Mrs. Burry, but that day, it only made Mrs. Burry feel sympathy— sympathy for what others feared.

There were three stalls. The younger woman went into the handicapped stall at the end. This was fine, Mrs. Burry thought. After all, she felt fully capable of using any stall, and she went into the first. She pushed, and the door opened easily, welcoming her.

"Thank you, door," Mrs. Burry mouthed silently, and with her dress, she sat down on the toilet. For a moment, Mrs. Burry forgot where she was and what she was about to do, and then she remembered: she had to use the toilet. She stood up, lifted her rumpled dress, which had no undergarments underneath, and sat back down. As she went to the bathroom, she closed her eyes. For how long, she did not know, but the sound of the running faucet startled her back into consciousness.

Whoever had used the faucet, maybe the woman in her forties, maybe someone else altogether, left it dripping. *Plink. Plink. Plink.* Into the metal basin. Mrs. Burry needed to shut it off. The water told her it didn't want to be wasted.

She flushed the toilet and stood. She clutched her purse and felt the bottles inside.

"Probably best to take another pain pill—just in case," she said. "All this moving around. I need to stay on top of it." She opened the red-capped bottle and put a pain pill in her mouth.

"Another can't hurt," she added.

In front of the sink, Mrs. Burry turned off the leaky faucet and then remembered she needed to swallow the pills in her mouth.

She tossed the pain pills into her mouth. She turned on the cold tap, cupped her wrinkled, veiny hands, and scooped more water into her mouth. She leaned back and swallowed. One soggy pill caught in the back of her throat, so she scooped more water up and into her throat. Swallowed again. This time, all pills were down.

Someone else pulled open the door. It was her cousin. Birdie's forehead was furrowed and sweaty.

"You've been gone some time," Birdie said with concern. "We have a table now," she added.

Mrs. Burry turned, half-smiled, and looked quizzically at Birdie.

"Eat? I haven't been this hungry in ages!" Mrs. Burry said. She stepped too quickly towards her cousin and lost her balance once again. She fell to the floor and hit her right hip.

"Oh!" gasped Birdie. "Really, maybe we should just go. Stay here. I'll get someone to help get you up."

Mrs. Burry didn't feel any pain. If anything, she felt sorry for the battered floor. Before Birdie came back with the hostess, Mrs. Burry had gotten back on her feet.

"I feel good, Birdie. Really. Let's not leave," Mrs. Burry pleaded.

Birdie took Mrs. Burry's arm and led her to the table. Mrs. Burry sat with her back to the wall, and Birdie and Bill faced her. It was a table for four, but when their waiter realized there were only three, he took away the extra plate, cup, silverware, and napkin. Mrs. Burry did not notice.

Both Birdie and Bill ordered coffee. Black. When the waiter asked what Mrs. Burry would like, Mrs. Burry announced, "A mimosa." Mrs. Burry hadn't had anything to drink since starting treatment, but she felt daring. She straightened her crinkled violet lace dress under the table and slid her feet out of her satin pumps so she could feel the carpet beneath. She sat up straight in the chair pushing out her chest, and she ran her right hand over her face and bald head where her hair used to be.

"Stay here," Birdie said. "We'll get you a plate."

"How lovely of you," Mrs. Burry said. She was enjoying the feel of the thin, looped carpet under her feet. "Everything," Mrs. Burry said. "I want to taste everything."

Across the room sat a young girl. Just one of many children. This one had dark blonde hair that was split down the middle and braided down both sides. She had pierced ears and looked to be in fourth or fifth grade. The young girl's dress was violet as well, but had no lace. It probably didn't have a slit up the back, either, and the young girl certainly didn't have the breasts to fill it out like Mrs. Burry did.

They looked at one another.

The girl raised her right hand and pointed to her own head. Then the girl raised both shoulders as if to ask "Why?"

Mrs. Burry answered with a look of confusion and pawed at the metal base of the table with her feet.

The waiter brought the mimosa, and Mrs. Burry drank it quickly, before her cousin and her cousin's husband returned with three plates of food.

"I'm so glad you have an appetite," Birdie said.

Mrs. Burry smiled and began to eat. The eggs were scrambled and watery, but they managed to taste like the best she ever had. Then the waffle, which brimmed with syrup. When she about to start on her bacon, she saw the little girl from across the room get up.

Abruptly, Mrs. Burry stood in her bare feet and said, "I'll be right back."

"Where are you…" Birdie began.

Mrs. Burry interrupted her. "I need to use the little girl's room. I mean the ladies' room. Again."

This time, Mrs. Burry knew to pull, not push, and easily entered the bathroom with three stalls and a leaky faucet. She spread her uncovered toes out wide on the cool tile floor and took a satisfying, deep breath.

The little girl was in the handicap stall, so Mrs. Burry went into the one next to it—even though she did not have to use the bathroom. Again, she sat in her dress on the toilet. Her head felt heavy, and she leaned it against the side of the stall separating her from the girl.

"Little girl," Mrs. Burry said.

"Are you talking to me?" the quiet voice answered.

"Yes," Mrs. Burry said.

"I'm not supposed to talk to strangers. Mommy said so."

"But I'm not a stranger. You saw me. You motioned to me. I'm the one who was sitting across the room from you."

"Oh," the girl blurted out. "Yes!"

"What is it you were trying to ask me?"

"Why are you bald?"

"Bald?" Then Mrs. Burry remembered: she _was_ bald. She _was_ sick. She had ailments that would never go away. Her husband left her. She was dying.

"I've been sick, but I'm not today."

"What do you mean you're not?" and the little girl flushed the toilet.

"Not today. My doctors gave me medicine, so I would be okay," and Mrs. Burry flushed too even though she had not gone.

The little girl and Mrs. Burry opened their stall doors at the same time.

Mrs. Burry asked, "Do you want to touch it?"

The girl nodded. Mrs. Burry bent over; the little girl petted the head no one else touched.

"Your eyes are really droopy," the girl added.

"What's your name?" Mrs. Burry asked, slurring even more as the pain pills exploded in her veins.

"Ivy. Ivy Madison. My mom said not to talk to strangers, but you're a bald stranger, so I think it's okay."

"I think I need to sit. Would you sit? Sit and talk with me?"

The little girl nodded.

They sat down against the wall opposite the sink.

"What's your name?" Ivy asked.

"Lillian."

"I'm not supposed to call old ladies by their first name."

"You can call me that, Ivy. I give you special permission." Lillian leaned her head against the cool bathroom wall, closing her eyes.

"I'm sad you're sick," Ivy said.

"Sick?" Lillian replied. "I have been, but I don't feel sick now, Ivy. Really, I feel good."

"What were you sick with?" Ivy, who was on the ground next to her, turned her head to look right into Lillian's eyes.

"Cancer."

"My uncle had cancer," Ivy said. "He died. Cancer is really bad, right?"

"It can be."

"Who is taking care of you?"

"My husband." There was a pause. "Wait. Not my husband. He left, Ivy. I'm on my own."

Saying that hurt, and Lillian reached for her violet sequin purse—still pregnant with the paraphernalia of sickness.

Ivy watched as Lillian took out three more pain pills. She didn't remember taking two just thirty minutes before. This time, she used the little saliva left in her mouth to swallow the three. The muscular walls of her esophagus struggled to pull them down to her stomach.

Just then, Birdie pulled open the door.

"What are you doing?" asked Birdie with alarm.

"I feel great! I'm not leaving, Birdie," she added.

"You're not what? Please!" Birdie urged.

"Don't make her go," Ivy said. "She has cancer. She feels good here. We should let her stay."

Birdie let the door close behind her and went to get her husband.

"Lock the door, Ivy," Lillian directed firmly. "You understand what I need, but they… they do not."

Ivy did what Lillian told her.

"It's locked," Ivy said, and she sat back down.

Lillian felt relieved.

"You are so good to me, floor," Lillian said.

"Are you talking to me?" Ivy asked.

"No, the floor, Ivy. I'm talking to the floor. You can, too. You just don't know it. What do you want to tell it? To say?"

Ivy didn't know what Lillian was talking about.

"Lillian, I'd like to go now."

Just then, there was pounding on the door.

"Ivy? Are you in there? It's Mommy. Are you okay?" Ivy looked up at the door with alarm.

Then Birdie spoke. "It's time to unlock the door. Did you lock yourself in there? Please come out. Everything will be okay. Just come out."

Lillian's face was expressionless.

"I don't want to be mean, but you look a zombie right now, Lillian," Ivy said.

"You're silly, Ivy," and then Lillian laughed as she began to see zombie versions of herself in the wallpaper, the ceiling tiles, the grout between the tile floors.

Ivy stood up and walked towards the door. "Lillian, my mommy is calling, and I'd like to unlock the door."

"No!" Lillian said. She unsteadily dove towards the door—in between it and Ivy.

Ivy started to cry.

"I just need another pill. Then it'll all be okay."

Lillian reached into her purse and found the Alisomb. She popped one. Then two. Crushing them with her teeth before gagging them down.

Lillian's problems were almost gone—all except the voices through the door and the crying little girl. Was there one girl or two? Were there more girls in the stalls? She started to check each one.

"Open the door, Ivy!" Ivy's mother ordered.

Ivy stopped crying. "Lillian, I don't think you want to hurt me."

Lillian looked at Ivy. "No, I don't, Ivy. I'll open the door for you, okay? But I need you to run out quickly because you understand what I need."

"I do," Ivy replied.

Lillian walked over to the door and stood behind it. She motioned for Ivy to unlock the door.

"I'm coming, Mommy." Ivy said. There was no response from the other side.

By then, there were sirens. They were getting closer. Lillian liked the sound: a repetitive refrain growing louder and louder.

Ivy unlocked the door, pushed it open, and ran out.

Just then, Lillian pushed the silver metal handle back in and quickly locked the door.

"We did it," Lillian said with satisfaction.

The sirens grew closer.

"More," Lillian said as she stumbled towards the sink and took out more pills. More would make them go away for good. More would erase the cancer that had spread to her bones. More would bring back her husband. Make her hair grow long. Make her breasts perky and whole.

Tiferet

She couldn't tell how many pills she had taken. She slumped to the floor and crawled to the handicapped stall.

"Another pill," she muttered before closing her eyes in a place where God had returned.

POETRY

The Garden At Sunset

C.W. Buckley

The man raised hard-packed earth in a patch around his ankles
Clearing knotted ivy-root with a dull pick-axe
That something yet unborn to him may take root and grow

An unruly hedge that rained juniper's blue-flame berries once
On the heads of his long-ago boys, he trimmed
Back that morning to three trunks, austere and slender as saplings

He worked a symmetry adhering to some unspoken rule of gardeners
When he unearthed a wonder: a sphere, curiously light,
Of stone he imagined might contain a geode

One spelunk! of his heavy tool into that tiny crystal cave
Would deliver its hues unto the sun at last
But he decided against it, fearing lumbar pain and the mess

Besides his wife expected the yard raked clean by dusk.
He tossed the orb, arcing it over gravel to lawn
Almost smelling the rising green to spread from where it came to rest

NONFICTION

Living the Three R's - Rejection, Reconciliation, Renewal

Victoria Waddle

> *The really vital question for us all is, What is this world going to be? What is life eventually to make of itself?*
>
> *-- William James, Pragmatism*

As a child, I had two great fears. The first was of a nuclear holocaust, a terror engendered in our regular duck-and-cover drills. Even as a child I knew the drills could not protect us from the blistered, weeping flesh that black and white educational films brought to life. Irradiation was our collective destiny. That the mutual annihilation we learned about was based upon ideological differences was something I was too young to understand. Now that the specter of the Reds has been replaced with religious zealotry, the old worry of annihilation over ideological differences returns. In the United States, school children are again practicing hiding in their classrooms because school shootings have become unexceptional. In other areas of the world, grenades are lobbed through classroom windows and girls are shot on school buses. Ideological differences—call them economic, political, or religious—continue to be the basis of all our fears.

Religious ideology was also the basis of my second great fear, one far more personal. My father wasn't much of a believer—I suppose he was more agnostic than atheist. He would drop my mother, my four siblings, and I off at the stained-glass Catholic Church, and then sit in the faux wood-trim station wagon and read the Sunday *Times* until we were finished. That he was destined for Hell there was no doubt. Unbaptized, he was not allowed to receive the body of Christ in the form of the Catholic Communion sacrament. All the sins of his life were upon him—he had never confessed, never had a single transgression absolved.

When I got the courage to ask my mother about my father's predicament, she told me that there was baptism of desire—that no one knows what is in another's heart, and that my father may have received Christ there. I was pretty small, but I knew she was fudging. (No, you couldn't call your mother a liar back then.) I could see that my dad was giving up his eternal glory for the chance to have an hour and a half alone to read the paper.

When we stopped the duck-and-cover drills, my fear of a nuclear blast dimmed. My religious fears—of a punishing, petty God—lasted much longer. I continued to pray each night ("If I die before I wake, I pray the Lord my soul to take") and kept my hands folded in case I did die because someone told me that would keep the mortician from having to break my fingers to pose them for the open casket. I reviewed the terrible things I had done and not been able to confess yet. I might well be scorched by the forever flames because I had called my brother a jerk and hadn't yet had a priest tell me to say ten Hail Marys.

That I took too much to heart a canon now either laughed off by the faithful or condemned by the apostate is evident. I am grown. Some of my religious training has fallen out of my life; much of it I have quite purposefully rejected. After several attempts to reconcile myself to the church that so carefully instilled those beliefs, I abandoned Catholicism altogether.

It's a simple enough statement to say that one has left her church. Before I did so, I had dark decades of the soul. My mother once told me that our religion was the foundation of our lives and that each person could rebuild the home that stands upon it.

Finally walking away felt like I had not only taken a wrecking ball to the ancestral cottage residing in my soul, in the soul of the family, but like I had pulled up the underpinning as well. That I worried I would have nothing left to build upon was what had kept me so long in hope of reconciliation rather than outright rejection. When news coverage broke about the Church's cover-ups of child molestation, I abandoned that hope.

It took time to realize how solidly my faith remained after I renounced my doctrine. When I read C. S. Lewis's *Mere Christianity*, I realized that I no longer met the simplest criteria that define a Christian. Yet, as I read works by the Dalai Lama, I agreed with him: Christianity is a wonderful religion when the practitioner adheres to the principals of Christ. Someone raised in those principals need not seek a religion outside her culture. I had spent more than enough of my life in self-flagellation. It was time to allow that I had been given some valuable lessons in my youth and that I was, at my core, a good person.

I now think of myself as a heretical Christian. I suppose this is what some people mean when they say—as they often do—"I'm not religious, but I'm spiritual." Because what remains—the sense of immersion in the glory of God—is almost impossible to define. A specific creed is so much easier to outline for others, making it common for people to think they can explain and defend their faith. Yet

Tiferet

William James evokes both Isaiah (55:8) and Job (40:4) in *Pragmatism* when he says, "God's ways are not our ways, so let us put our hands upon our mouth." Even that there can be great joy in seeking after a discipline of righteousness makes for difficult translation. Recently, in reconnecting with an old college friend, I mentioned that I was reading *Moral Evil* by Andrew Michael Flescher. He lowered his eyebrows, cocked his head at me and said, "You used to be fun."

If we can't expect to be fully understood by people known to us, how do we get along with those who appear unknowable? It is a truism that most violence done throughout history has been perpetrated in the name of religion. Yet this is too broad a statement. The damage done to me by religion was actually done through what appeared to be a "gotcha" dogma of impossible rules and a demand to worship, without question, an unappeasable God with no basis in the example of Christ. What religion taught me that *did* adhere to the Christian example—the golden rule, the lessons of the parables, the sense of the "I" and the terrifying, fascinating, numinous "Thou"—have been equally the discomposure and the joy of my soul. They have created purpose and expression in my life as a mother, and in my career as an educator.

My experience is hardly unique. I understand that our push for peace can't be arbitrary, and yet I sense that it is still unmapped. Like Colum McCann's Irish monk, John Corrigan, in the novel, *Let the Great World Spin*, I believe that the space we hold for God is the last frontier. Like William James, I cannot imagine we will ever map that territory in a unified set of religious rules:

> Whoever claims absolute teleological unity, saying that there is one purpose that every detail of the universe subserves, dogmatizes at his own risk. Theologians who dogmatize thus find it more and more impossible, as our acquaintance with the warring interests of the world's parts grows more concrete, to imagine what the one climacteric purpose may possibly be like.

I often take walks in my local wilderness. This is, perhaps, an inept description—my hills are full of heat and crispy chaparral nearly done in by drought. In the tradition of the Desert Fathers and Mothers, I find this a perfect environment for contemplation. Recently, in pondering religious differences and difficulties, my mind tracked to James Bond, a seeming diversion. Suave and smart, Bond has a child's worship of his boss M., and would do anything for him, even if it works outside the bounds of his ethic. Bond will wreak vengeance upon M's personal enemies to have his boss's approval.

Perhaps my sudden thoughts of Bond are not as weird as they first seemed. In religion, there has always been a key group of people willing to violate the core commands of their faith ("Love one another as I have loved you;" the wealthy's duty to help the needy; that one should not harm himself or others, etc.) in order to curry favor with unethical leaders or modern prophets. Sometimes this mind-meld with evil shepherds ends in the tragedy of terrorism.

Thinking of Bond's boss, I remembered reading, only days before, the distracted grief and winding talismans of purpose in Patti Smith's *M Train*. In this autobiographical work, Smith concludes that "life is at the bottom of things and belief is at the top, while the creative impulse, dwelling in the center, informs all." While I would have said that the opportunity for a free-thinking education is the necessary element in a coming together of various faiths, I am in line with Smith. It's difficult to avoid some set of rules. (When two or more are gathered together, you'd better have some norms.) Yet for religion to evolve into a completely fearless faith, it must welcome exploration by its adherents despite the very real risk that such seeking will lead to its rejection. A willingness to risk rejection is the basis of all good relationships. It lays the foundation for true acceptance.

And, yes, as Tom Petty once sang, the waiting is the hardest part. In a recent article in the liberal Christian magazine *Sojourners*, author Katharine M. Preston laments, "I am impatient: Why can't the arc of the moral universe run, rather than just bend, toward justice?"

Still, progress has been made—enslavement of others is no longer taught from Christian pulpits. Even the far less evil catechisms I so feared as a child have fallen away. If we are to continue to move forward in our—often painfully slow—coming together, we must understand that unbelief is not the end of faith. Despair is the end of faith, and we must not despair. "For now we see through a glass, darkly; but then face-to-face: now I know in part; but then shall I know even as also I am known" (1 Corinthians 13:12).

FICTION

On The Hook

Siamak Vossoughi

One day when he was thirteen years old, Khosro Daneshvar went to his father and said, "Baba, you don't have to know the answers to things anymore."

What he meant was that he was not dealing in things that had answers anymore. Why was there sorrow and meanness in the world? Why were men and women unhappy? Why was life so far away? These were his concerns now. They were questions he wanted to keep as questions.

He wanted his father to know that he was off the hook.

His father didn't know what to make of being off the hook.

Have I been overburdening him with answers, he thought. He liked to think of himself as a man with some answers, though he didn't think he had many more or less than the next man. Certainly a man has to have *some* answers, perhaps especially a man who is a father, he thought.

He thought he liked it better when he was on the hook.

His son was quieter now, but every once in a while he would look at his father and smile sadly as if he was taking some solace in the fact that his father didn't have to worry about answers anymore.

The smile terrified him.

"What?" he would say.

"Nothing," Khosro would say.

His father felt that what answers he'd given him so far were small. He went over them in his head: Be nice to your little sister. Work hard in school. Listen to your mother. They were fine enough answers, but the boy already did those things, so he didn't know how useful it was to state them anymore.

The next time his father saw his own brother, he asked him if any of his children had ever told him than he didn't have to worry about answers anymore.

"No," his brother said. "They've told me not to bother them with questions, though."

Khosro's father thought he would rather his son had told him not to bother him with questions. That was the kind of thing you could expect from a boy of thirteen, at least.

"He has told you that you don't have to worry about answers anymore?" his brother said.

"Yes. He does not say it angrily, though."

"How does he say it?"

"Like I am off the hook."

"Off the hook?"

"Yes."

"Were you on the hook before?"

"Yes. I think so."

"Well," his brother said. "You should make the most of being off the hook."

Khosro's father did not know how to make the most of it. It was a very lonely feeling to be off the hook. That night, he got the idea that if he couldn't be on the hook, then somebody could be, and that somebody could be Khosro. He began to wonder aloud about all kinds of things around his son. He wondered about small things and he wondered about big things. He wondered about life and he wondered about death.

His son listened. He didn't offer any answers but he listened. Pretty soon he began to wonder aloud as well. His father was very happy to hear it. But he did not jump to answers. Nobody was on the hook between them and nobody was off it either. Instead, they both secretly trembled to see that a father and son wondering together was answer enough.

NONFICTION

Convicted

Allison Schuette

I don't know where the conviction came from. Seemingly, I arrived, the belief sewn into the inner lining of my genetic material. *I deserve a life free from pain.* I don't pretend to be unique—although I do know those who, through means healthy or otherwise, have accommodated themselves to the reality that pain cannot or need not be avoided. I mention this now in order to study the tenacity of my conviction, the way the belief holds me enthralled despite all the evidence that might prove me wrong.

The key lies, as with most sentences, in the verb. When pain arrives, the interrogative voice sneaks up on me: *What have I done to deserve this*? And that quickly, I move from event—the hard-packed material of external reality—to behavior and moral assessment.

***

When K. admitted to falling in love with someone else the first time, I assumed the strength of our relationship and the weight of our sixteen-year history would pull us through. Plus, M. was the one who pursued him. I understand now, though, that in letting her pursue him, he created the chase.

On the night in which K confessed his love for M to me, he'd brought her to our house. This despite the fact that I had told him something about her troubled me, something I couldn't yet put my finger on; and until such time as I could, would he please not invite her home?

From the earliest years of our relationship, I believed that I had a problem sharing K with others. Since I was used to being the sole focus of his attention, when he showed an interest in someone else, I assumed that implied a loss of interest in me. This logic troubled me. Where had I gotten the idea that we each had a finite reservoir of interest? Did I not have other friends that I cared for without experiencing any loss of desire for K? And what exactly did it mean to enjoy being the sole focus of someone's attention? Such fixation lay at the heart of romance, but an authentic relationship surely had reason to question such a saccharin ideal.

I didn't know what to do about the nagging intuition that told me something felt wrong in these situations, but I assumed it was my problem. K did not suggest otherwise.

If some sixteen years into our relationship, I still wrestled with the same issues, I didn't expect K to change his behavior. I did expect him, however, to respect the way in which I needed to deal with it. So when he went out with M that night for drinks, I prepared myself for a long night. I knew I wouldn't be able to sleep until he got home, and I knew that might be well past midnight. When I heard the truck return at nine-thirty, I chastised myself. *See, you worried over nothing.* But when M and K walked in the house together with a case of beer, my heart plummeted. I tried to catch K's eye. He walked past me on the way into the kitchen. "We forgot it was Saint Patrick's Day. The bars are so full we couldn't hear a word the other said." The bottles clinked as he put the beer in the fridge.

I stayed up with them for about an hour and then withdrew to bed, tired and hoping against hope I'd be able to sleep. When I heard him on the stairs around midnight, I chastised myself again. I took a deep breath and realized that I had been holding it for the last hour.

But he was only coming for clothing.

"It's cold in the basement."

"Take her home," I replied.

"Just one more drink."

"You know how I feel."

"Just one more, Al."

I didn't stay in bed the whole time. I sneaked down the stairs as quietly as I could, twice, to eavesdrop at the vent above the basement. I heard their voices, but not exactly what they said. I felt ridiculous, dirty.

K came upstairs a few hours later. I'd left my bedside light on while I floated between restless sleep and reading whatever I had at hand. K stopped and stood near the foot of the bed, head hung low.

"I think I'm in love with her."

***

The dream does not begin that night; it begins several years later, when K falls in love again. In the dream, I cannot find him anywhere. I frantically search, believing that if only I can talk to him, I can change the outcome. This belief is so tenuous, I must focus my entire will on its assertion. The strength this requires simultaneously makes me powerful and weak. I refuse to look at the weakness, to recognize that I cannot sustain this.

There must be a way. There must be.

I invent hope without acknowledging its invention. Some part of myself— the will that represses, the will that refuses—works outside my conscious awareness, casting the lure of hope far out over the river of my desire, drawing me forward.

Anyone listening carefully can hear the fishing line sing.

***

I left the house early the next morning, before M woke up. K had set her up in the basement the night before. "How could you?" I'd asked. He didn't understand my sense of alienation, didn't get that the resonance of their illicit evening now lay more deeply lodged in the material being of this house that had been ours, just ours, a house we opened and shared with others but one that always came back to us. Its physical reality was entwined with an exclusive emotional connection. K didn't see the relationship between the physical and the emotional, or he refused to. For him, M's presence in the basement was the practical result of a late night spent drinking— how could he have sent her home?

"Come here," he'd said and pulled me to him in bed. "Let's just sleep. We'll talk more tomorrow."

I'd wanted this, wanted him to want to comfort me, and I took it for what it was worth. But something else—electric, sibilant—lay lodged between us.

***

I didn't lose trust in K right away. Relief came first; my intuition had been right. The unease I'd always experienced around M had a source. All the gut wrenching of that particular night had not been invented. And he had confessed. Now his feelings were out in the open and we could talk about them.

To this day, the seduction of hope, its power, confounds me.

Do not confuse hope with faith. Faith has no knowledge of outcomes. It allows you to sit with pain, knowing this too shall pass, if not how or when. Hope, on the other hand, is a form of desire, a pull towards a particular outcome that rests so close to anticipation, in its name you will tolerate almost anything. Hope avoids present pain by conjuring a future in which you will not hurt.

***

K fell in love the second time two years later. I watched his friendship with R develop. Initially, I celebrated and encouraged it, pleased that I finally didn't feel threatened by K's interest in another person. And R wanted to be my friend, too. She came to me for advice—about sex of all things—because, she said, all her other friends were male. I saw from our encounters that she would always be closer to K— they had so much in common—but nothing in me hesitated. I thought perhaps I had finally evolved.

When R arrived on our doorstep late one night, distraught with a broken heart, I made her a grilled cheese and tea. I made up the basement sofa, insisting she stay the night. Together, K and I stayed up with her, took care of her.

Not much more than a month later, during a party K and I were hosting, I found K and R together in the basement completely absorbed in one another. Their behavior was, by all accounts, harmless, but there was a magnetic charge between them. If I had wanted to ask them to stop, to what would I have pointed? *Your proximity to each other makes me uncomfortable. Could you please stand apart?* When I did mention it later to K, all I could say was, "You just kept staring at her. It was as if I wasn't even there."

I threw my chapstick at him; it hit him in the chest. He stood there motionless, unblinking.

***

In the dream, crucifixion awaits me. I know I cannot escape this sentence, yet I run. No one really chases me; no one has to. My refusal to submit is what hounds me. The patience of those who have condemned me, their complete absence, only heightens the terror. They are so assured of their power they don't bother to assert my powerlessness. I can run as long as I want, but they know I will eventually accept my fate. They know that at some point I will experience acceptance as relief, that I will lie myself down upon the crossbeam. And because they know, I know, but I am so far from acceptance, I claw at air. I am refusal itself, wild and blind.

***

K denied anything was happening between him and R. For the entire summer, they would sit together beside the outdoor fire pit, where they knew I couldn't stay for long because of the mosquitos. When I went away for a three-day workshop, I promised myself I wouldn't call him—but when I did anyway, first at 10:00 p.m., then 11:00, and then, finally midnight, he never answered. Later, he explained that he didn't hear the phone because he had been outside with R.

R was part of everything we did that summer; even the tupperware party. My friend, J, and I had been planning the event since spring. Part-performance and part-social-history, the event included displays, a rope-and-clothespin timeline strung across the ceiling, readings, old cookbooks, and Jell-O salads. I couldn't stop R from coming, even though I wanted to. I knew that if I raised the issue, K would say: *what is she going to think if you uninvite her? You'll just make her uncomfortable.* She arrived early with a sign she had made for the party. K laughed, delighted, and took her downstairs to find the tools they needed to plant it in the yard. I hated her.

I had to split my consciousness in order to enjoy the evening at all. I trained part of it to attend to guests and to take pleasure with J in what we had created. The other part watched while K sat on the porch with R, picking at the guitar. They weren't alone, but they were so centered on each other that the others drifted off soon enough.

R tried to stay at the end of the evening to help with the dishes. When I remember that moment, I see myself standing between the two of them at the sink, literally cleaving them apart. Really, I probably did nothing more than insist several times, "No, we don't need help. Thanks for everything. No, really, I'm giving you a ride home." When I returned, K, still at the sink, wouldn't speak to me. He lashed out and slammed the door on his way out for a cigarette when I probed him.

***

I want to have been heroic. I wish I had kicked K out of the house early that summer. In that vision, I circumvent pain. It's all over the moment I tell K to go, as soon as I affirm my worth, demanding that he does, too. My rosy chest bursts with integrity and conviction. I armor myself in its righteousness.

Of course, this vision is a lie. No amount of integrity protects us from pain. Integrity resides in the ability to hold pain. Pema Chödrön, an American Buddhist nun, writes that pain is not punishment and pleasure is not reward. She also writes that to desire a life free from pain is to long for death.

Even if I could have stopped the pain by taking action earlier, should I have? At what cost? I kept hope as long as I did because I loved K, because I wanted a life with him. My willingness to remain vulnerable might itself have been heroic. What kind of monster would I be without pain? What kind of martyr?

***

Two memories have burned themselves into my mind.

One: it is summer. K is assisting with communion. We are gathered in the Gloria Christi chapel, a small, intimate space. R rises to receive communion. I watch the way K offers her the cup and grasps her hands in his. This is not a gesture he has ever made toward me, a reality made more painful now by the memory of his revelation some three years back that when I had been away at graduate school, he had prayed every time the host landed on his ring that God would call me back to the faith, that he and I would once again be able to share this religious tradition.

Two: the three of us are at the house together. As usual, I have orchestrated the end of the evening. I would have ended it hours earlier, but I waited until my stomach could no longer take it, until the anxiety threatened to crush my throat. In an effort at appearing capacious, bullying myself into believing nothing is going on, I always let K say goodnight to R outside. But tonight my patience has worn thin. I step out back to smoke a cigarette and tell myself that by the time I have finished, R will be gone. But halfway through the cigarette, I realize I can't do it. I circle around to the front of the house. Illuminated by the light of the front porch, K and R are kissing. "I am not okay with this," I declare. I deny R her panic as she stumbles backwards into a crying fit. I use her guilt to force her home.

Later, after our separation, after K chooses R, after I finalize the divorce, I draw these memories on paper to exorcise them. It is one of the first ways I give shape to the pain in order to accept it.

***

I wake up before the inevitability of the dream occurs. I have chased myself through city streets, encountered K's parents, propelled myself up the grassy knoll where three crosses stand. There's a heartbeat like the pounding of a hammer. Everything in me retreats even as the form of my person walks forward. I dredge myself upward out of the dream, force my panic to take the shape of this ceiling, these skylights, the closet doors, my cats curled into me, and the empty pillow on the other side of the bed.

Tiferet

POETRY

Loveladies

(for Basho)

JoAnn Bertelo

All along the road
at the end of this island
summer sounds simmer and scatter,
kayaks patter
waves silent shatter
crystal sun.

My bicycle,
bell ringing,
basket filled full with fresh stone fruit
and lavender bouquets.

This soft sultry summer could last all day.
Only autumn evening comes

Alex Lang   IMPERFECT METAPHOR

NONFICTION

All the Rage (Excerpt)

Martin Moran

I am standing in the living room of my Manhattan apartment holding a receiver attached to a phone wired to the wall. I'm glad for the grounded line, the grip of the thing, as I hear myself say,

"Could you please connect me to the police, the police station for Goleta, California?"

It is early in the year 2006. Drifts of muddied snow are dwindling in the warmth beyond the window. I don't recall crossing from my desk through our living room to pick up the telephone. It's happened as if in a dream, yet now the real voice, the flat vowels, the well-mannered melody of a middle-American operator:

"Please hold, sir, for the Goleta Sheriff's Department."

"Thank you, ma'am."

The public school kids are out in the sun across the street. Jackets tied at the waist; tossed to the foot of the fence. My eyes stay out the window toward the sky-blue day, the swirl of little bodies on the playground, as I wait for the cross continent connection. Wait through a distant crackle, then a long stretch of silence linking itself to the law of the land in California. I was at the desk paying bills? Composing sentences? Now, suddenly, pressing the receiver to my head to keep from hanging up, a thumping heart betraying an old fear, an old ache to make right what went wrong.

It's ringing.

I am picturing a small town. Rural. I've never been there. I know it only as the return address scribbled on a long ago letter sent to me by Bob. I have no idea if he still lives there; if he still lives.

It's ringing and a tantrum rises up in my chest: Hang up! Questions hammering: *What are you afraid of? The derision of a sheriff? That you're betraying your old buddy Bob? That he might hurt or threaten you? For Christ's sake, you're nearly fifty, kid. Talk about Stockholm Syndrome.*

"Hello. Sheriff's office."

It's a woman on the line and I'm instantly relieved. What I wish to say I think will be easier to reveal to a her. And she repeats:

"Sheriff's office."

"Hello. My name is Martin Moran and…" My voice quavers from whiskerless boy to man of fifty. "I am calling because I think someone may reside there who molested me when I was a kid."

I'm aware in this instant how the news of my friend Ben's death, some months before, is part of the impetus for this call, this reaching back. What happened to Ben was more brutal I figure than what happened to me. At least Bob didn't ply me with liquor and fuck me in the ass. Nonetheless…

"Yes. How can I help you?" The sheriff asks.

"I just wanted to be sure that you were aware of his…him."

How matter of fact I suddenly sound.

"Was he ever convicted?" she asks.

"Yes, Ma'am. In Colorado. In the Seventies," I say, thinking (again) how someone else did that brave work. "Not by me, though, Ma'am."

I hear my voice lilting upward against the weight of an adage (the heft of Edmund Burke) lodged in my brain somewhere along the way.

The only thing necessary for evil to triumph
is for good men to do nothing.

Nothing is what I did.

Easy now. You were a kid, kid. You were a kid.

"His name?" she asks.

"Robert Kosanke."

I say it aloud to her and I type it now for you (for me) in black letters on a white page. Tabloid style.

Robert Kosanke.

The name. The real, the actual, the seven-letter nonfiction name.

In my memoir released in 2005, I recount the story of my sexual entanglement with Kosanke. 'Bob.' The guy who pulled me into his sleeping bag at a boys summer camp a few months after my twelfth birthday, the illicit sex ending when I was a freshman in high school. I also created a stage version of my story, a dramatic monologue rendering the essentials: Catholic upbringing, the molestation at twelve, finding and confronting Bob thirty years later. In the book I called him, Robert C___. I didn't want to ruffle any feathers, to sully my poetry with his sullied name. I didn't want a harangue but an inquiry. And I liked (still do) the space, the invitation for the reader to fill in the blank with their very own ghost, their private nemesis. And the little dash of emptiness—of mystery—reminds me of the stories of an earlier time ("Josef K_ was dreaming. It was a beautiful day and K_ felt like going for a walk."), by an Old World author like, for instance, Kafka. The little void that hums of a dark fable, a fable that reminds you how you'll never quite know, never totally understand, the whole story. Even if you're the one who lived it, the one who's attempting to remember, to tell it. I believed that without the weight of his factual name, without the business of blame, the narrative could rise toward the grace and forgiveness it was seeking. That's what I wished (then), and that's what I set out to compose—a kid's hymn to freedom, a man's ode to compassion.

And besides, the publisher's legal counsel felt it prudent to alter identifying names and details. Ah, a comfort to have my Catholic School Courtesy, my aesthetic choice, seconded by literary-legal opinion.

OK.

So.

Here I am now, spelling out *Kosanke*. And I confess that doing so rings a bit of belated redress. Is this the bitter thrill of vengeance, I wonder? An admission of my abiding desire for payback? Do I like the idea that somewhere, someone who knows him (he himself?) will feel the sting of seeing the true name in print? Even as I worry the sting will hurt others, him, or even as I wonder if stinging him is part of freeing me and fuck it. Is that what I'm after at this late date? A step, a stab, a slap that I missed, a jot of justice that will help to put the whole mess to rest?

If so, so be it.

Or, is this ink you now see (this phone call I recount) simply a long-deferred civic duty? A small but important effort to protect others.

"Still checking," the lady says. I hear the clicking sound of what must be her fingernails on a keyboard. I am picturing a small street, a ramshackle house; a truck in the drive up on a jack, missing a wheel, tools scattered in a driveway, weeds creeping through cracked cement. I picture him gray and slow and bent as he was when I finally found and faced him one afternoon in 2002 at a VA hospital in California. He told me then how he fixed up old cars for a meager living and I imagine him now asking a neighbor boy to help change a tire on the old Chevy, to step inside for a spot of lemonade.

"Yes... yes, he does live here," she finally says.

"So, he's alive?" I ask, amazed that a phone call was all it took to confirm this fact, and disappointed, I realize, that he's not dead. Always guessing that death (his or mine) would be the certain period on this story. The story that apparently (for here I am again at the keyboard typing "Bob") refuses to end.

"Yes, we know where he is," she continues, with a kind of Perry Mason delivery. "He is a *registrant*."

"What's that?"

"He's required by law to register with us periodically. It's part of his agreement. He is current, I see."

"So you're aware, I mean, able to—"

`"Yes, sir. We keep an eye."

The relief! Someone is doing the job of stopping him. The job I never did. How many slim blonde boys came after me? How many like Ben?

"Anything else I can help you with?"

"Ah, no. No. Thank you so much. Thank you."

"Well, thanks for your call, Martin." Her voice is kindness. "Take good care, now."

My throat tightens, my eyes well up.

She understands, I think. *She understands everything.*

It took me thirty years to call the cops.

FICTION

Mr. Clean

Lesléa Newman

When the doorbell rings I glance at the digital clock on the nightstand with the tall, skinny neon green numbers we bought last month so that Marvin could see the time without his glasses. Nine-thirteen. Who on earth is ringing my bell so early on a Tuesday morning? Thank God I'm out of bed and dressed, which isn't the way it usually goes these days. Though I'm not exactly dressed. Sweat pants and one of Marvin's worn flannel shirts isn't my most fetching outfit. Not that it matters. Now that there's no one here to fetch.

I schlep myself over to the bedroom window and peer down at our front landing. And what do I see? A bird's eye view of the top of Burt's glossy head. Burt! Of course it's Burt. How could I forget? He's only been coming here every other Tuesday between nine o'clock and nine-fifteen for twenty-seven years.

"I'm coming," I call, though Burt can't possibly hear me. Slowly I lug myself across the bedroom, grasping onto the edge of dressers—first Marvin's, then mine—and then clinging to the doorjamb like a toddler who has recently learned to walk. It's been like this since last year when I fell and my hip snapped in half like the number two pencils I use to solve the crossword puzzles. They say I didn't fall and break my hip, my hip broke and that made me fall. Whatever. I'm still careful. I need another accident like I need a hole in the head.

Burt doesn't ring the bell again even though it's taking me longer than usual to get downstairs. Usually I'm waiting right by the front door for him. But nothing is usual these days. And what does Burt care? He's not in a hurry. He's never in a hurry. And he knows I'm home. Our shiny blue Nissan is in the driveway big as life, which means that Marvin and I….

Oh my God. Burt doesn't know.

My breath catches in my throat and my nose tingles like it does right before I cry. Though I haven't let myself cry during the past two weeks at all. "She's so brave. So strong," I heard over and over at the funeral. Don't they know I have to be strong? Don't they know if I start crying I won't be able to stop? *Hold it together, Doris*, I tell myself. *You can do this. You have to do this.* "Okay," I say to myself. I do that a lot lately. Tell myself it's okay. Which of course it isn't.

I sigh a deep sigh, which is another new habit, and make my way down the hallway, slow as Speedy, the turtle that Rhonda brought home when she was twelve. *Dorrie, let her keep it,* Marvin said. *It doesn't eat much and it doesn't shed.* Only Marvin could convince me to keep a prehistoric-looking reptile the size of a shoebox in the house. At least it wasn't a snake.

"I'm coming," I call again when I get to the top of the stairs. Which foot goes down first, the good one or the not-so-good one? I can never remember. *So try one and then try the other,* Marvin said when he brought me home from rehab. *The odds are with you, kiddo. You've got a fifty-fifty chance.*

Marvin! Will I always hear you kibitzing in my head like this? I certainly hope so. I don't think I can do this without you. *You can do it,* Marvin's raspy voice whispers. *Dorrie, you can do anything.*

No, I can't, I silently argue as I creep down the stairs, clutching the banister hand over hand. Before I open the door, I peer through the peephole, even though I know it's Burt. Still, one can't be too careful these days.

Burt's been coming to the house for decades, but still the sight of him takes me by surprise. Maybe it's the hair. It's jet black like the India Ink that Rhonda spilled her senior year in high school when she took up calligraphy. That stain has yet to come out of the pink shag carpet and she already has two kids older than she was at the time that it happened. I was furious, but Marvin shrugged it off. "It's only a rug," he said. "Leave it for now, and we'll replace it when she goes off to college." But for some reason, we never did.

Burt's hair is just like that stain. Unexpected and startling. Much too dark for a man his age. Plus it's thick and slicked back and it gleams in the sun like the marble countertops in the kitchen that he's come here to clean. Burt looks like an Elvis impersonator. A bad Elvis impersonator. I always expect him to say, "Well, hello little lady," when I open the door. He doesn't, of course. He says, "Good morning, Mrs. B. It's a gorgeous day, isn't it?" and gestures up at the sky with the nozzle of his vacuum cleaner. Then he gives me a smile so wide, I can practically see his tonsils. Burt's teeth have yellowed over time, like Marvin's old undershirts, the ones he never let me throw away, even when I brought home a brand new pack. "There's nothing wrong with the ones I have," he said. "Save your shekels." I suppose Burt can use Marvin's ratty old undershirts as shmates now. Except then I'd have to tell him.

"Come in, Burt," I force myself to say in a voice that isn't a shriek.

"Don't mind if I do." Burt tips an imaginary hat, a standing joke between us. He always waits for me to invite him inside, as if there's a chance I might turn him away like a Jehovah's Witness or one of those college-age boys in green polo shirts who are always coming around trying to sell me lawn care products. God forbid a Long Island lawn shouldn't be as perfectly green as the ping pong table in the basement which Rhonda begged and begged us for and then never used.

I hold open the screen door with one arm and rise up on my toes at the same time, making myself as skinny as possible so Burt can squeeze by with his vacuum cleaner and plastic bucket of cleaning supplies. I can just hear that physical therapist from rehab chirping at me: "Mrs. Bergman! Heels on the floor! Remember your balance! And where are your shoes?" She was always so doggedly cheerful, it was all I could do not to slap her.

"How are you, Burt?" I ask like I always do. Like nothing has changed.

"I'm fine, Mrs. B.," Burt says, glancing up into the living room where he usually finds Marvin hiding behind the Business section of the *Times*. "Where's Mr. B.?"

Where indeed? If Marvin was sitting there—if only!—he'd lower the paper and proclaim, "Well, well, well, if it isn't Mr. Clean!" which always made Burt smile. Little did he know that this was a joke between Marvin and me. Burt isn't exactly the world's greatest housecleaner. He never was, and now he's gotten worse, missing a spot of tomato sauce near the stove's back burner, or a tumbleweed of dust behind the living room couch. He probably needs glasses by now but is too vain to wear them. But he's such a nice guy, and he's been with us for so long, I could never bring myself to fire him.

"Mr. B is… he's… he's out," I say with a vague wave of my hand. *Out of this world,* I think to myself. "Mr. Goldstein picked him up. They went out for breakfast. To the diner. Marvin likes the blintzes there," I babble as if I need to explain to Burt how Marvin could possibly be out of the house with the car still parked in the driveway. It's not like there's anywhere to walk to around here. "And then they were going to the post office. And then a few other errands. I have a dress at the cleaners…"

Burt takes all this in without question—why should he question me?—and just stands there waiting, cleaning supplies in hand. I know what he's waiting for. "How was the traffic?" I ask.

"Not too bad," he answers. "I left the house early so I wouldn't be late. But I didn't have time for coffee."

"I was just going to make myself a cup," I lie, falling into our standard routine as if we're a well-rehearsed pair. Laurel and Hardy. Lucy and Ethel. "Would you like some?"

"If it isn't too much trouble," Burt replies.

"No trouble at all. Just as easy to make two cups as it is to make one," I say so he won't feel bad for asking. Though he didn't exactly ask. "Come with me."

Burt finally puts down his cleaning supplies and follows me through the saloon-type swinging doors into the kitchen. Marvin's bright idea. "Where do you think we are, the wild west?" I asked when we first bought the house and he insisted on installing them. "We moved from Brooklyn to Long Island, not New Mexico," I reminded him. "Giddy up," he answered with a playful slap on my behind. "Very funny," I huffed, pretending to be annoyed, which of course I wasn't. "Ride 'em, cowgirl," he said, gathering me into his arms. "Really, Marvin?" I said. "In the kitchen?"

"Why not?" he asked. "In the kitchen, in the living room, in the dining room…"

Don't go there, I warn myself. *You'll be sorry.*

I hear Burt shift his weight behind me, and realize I've completely forgotten about him. "Sit down," I gesture toward the breakfast nook and turn my back to make our coffee. I don't remember when this ritual of ours started. Maybe a year ago, maybe two? One day Burt told me that he didn't have time for his coffee before he left the house and then the next thing I knew, I was cooking him breakfast, sometimes toast and scrambled eggs, sometimes a bagel, and on top of that, cleaning up his crumbs when he was through. Marvin just shook his head with that bemused smile. "Only you, Dorrie," he said, "would wind up cleaning up after the cleaning man who, let me remind you, we hired to clean."

But what the heck. I don't mind, really. Burt has never said anything, but my guess is he can no longer afford to feed himself three meals a day. He lives in a one-room apartment in a not-so-great neighborhood in the Bronx, and I'm sure it's hard for him to scrape by. He hasn't raised his price in a good ten years. And everything else has gone up. Marvin and I have certainly had to cut back. Everyone has.

I take out a coffee filter (a "gefilte" Rhonda used to call them), pull the coffee grounds out of the freezer, and fill the back of our ancient Mr. Coffee with water from the tap.

"Are you hungry, Burt? Would you like a bagel?" I turn to him and freeze. Burt is sitting in Marvin's chair, with his legs spread out to here—why do all men sit like that?—leaning back like he doesn't have a care in the world. He always sits in Marvin's chair at the head of the table and it never bothered me before. But for the past two weeks, no one has dared to sit in Marvin's chair. Not the Rabbi who's come to visit three times and calls every day, such a mensch he is; not Rhonda, who stayed with me all that terrible first week until I told her, enough already, she should go home, she has her own life, somehow I'd manage; and not Rhonda's husband Terry, my charming, good-looking, but not-too-bright goyishe son-in-law who put a paper plate piled high with cold cuts down on one of the wooden boxes the temple sent over for us to sit on during our seven days of mourning. Even the grandchildren knew better than to plop themselves down in Papa's chair. For the entire week that we sat shiva, Marvin's chair remained empty, his absence so present, I kept seeing him out of the corner of my eye, the shadow of a ghost slumped at the kitchen table waiting for me to bring him a cup of tea.

"I don't want you to go to all that trouble," Burt says, and for a split second I don't know what he's talking about. Then I remember I asked if he wanted a bagel.

"I was just going to have one myself." Again I lie. I wonder if I'll be able to push a bite of bagel past the lump that has taken up residence in my throat and clearly intends to stay. For the past two weeks, all I've managed to gulp down for breakfast is half a bowl of high fiber cereal that tastes like wet straw. Anything else seems too hard to swallow and too difficult to make. I know I need to eat more—I lost so much weight in rehab, the food they served was from hunger, let me tell you—I came out of there weighing less than I did when I was a bride. "How do you like my girlish figure?" I asked Marvin with one hand on my newly mended but still fragile hip. He barely looked up from the Sports section. "Dorrie, we've been married for fifty-two years," he said as if this was news to me. "I couldn't care less about your figure." At first I thought he was being unkind, but then I realized he meant that he loved me no matter how much or how little I weighed. And I know I weigh too little. I really haven't eaten much in the past few weeks and I could stand to put on a few pounds, which is something I never thought I'd say in my entire life.

"Okay," I say softly to myself as I take two bagels out of a plastic bag. I drop one, then the other, into the bagel slicer we bought after Rhonda, trying to surprise Marvin and me by bringing us breakfast in bed one day, surprised herself by slicing the palm of her hand with our good serrated knife. "Did you know that bagel accidents are the number one cause for Sunday morning emergency room visits?" the handsome young doctor calmly told Marvin as he tended to Rhonda's angry-looking wound. "Is that so?" Marvin replied, feigning interest as Rhonda howled and I squeezed her non-injured hand.

The things that stick in your craw. I shake my head and place the bagel halves into the toaster oven, plug it in, and turn it on. Then I glance over at Burt, who has now snapped his legs shut, thank God, and is staring out the window at the apple tree Marvin never got around to pruning last spring. I wonder what Burt is thinking. We never really say much beyond small talk. Often we say nothing at all. Which, this morning, is perfectly fine with me.

I busy myself with breakfast, opening the refrigerator to hunt around for the I-Can't-Believe-It's Not-Butter, the low fat cream cheese with chives, the sugar-free apricot jam. The sight of a half-eaten extra large Hershey's Special Dark chocolate bar—Marvin's favorite treat—slays me every time I see it, but I can't bring myself to throw it away. Every night he ate exactly two squares after supper while he watched the news. "You have to have something sweet to balance out the bitter," he always said, giving himself an excuse to indulge. And who cared anymore about his diabetes? At the end, it was the least of our problems. If Marvin wanted to eat an entire chocolate cake and top it off with a hot fudge sundae I would have let him; he should only enjoy before the cancer got him. But the cancer didn't get him. His heart did. We didn't even know there was anything wrong with his heart. One day he has a funny feeling. We think maybe it's indigestion. He takes a Tums. Then another. Then some Pepto Bismol. Then he goes to sleep and the next morning he wakes up dead. Right next to me. But what do I know? I slip out of bed not to wake him—ha!—and put on the coffee. He doesn't come down, and he doesn't come down, so I go back up to tell him breakfast is ready and he's ice cold. That was the worst moment of my life. No, I take that back. Every moment since then has been the worst moment of my life. This one included.

Maybe I should just tell Burt to sit in a different chair. Maybe I should get rid of the chair. Maybe I should get rid of Marvin's old undershirts. Maybe I should take Marvin's voice off our answering machine. Maybe I should crawl back into bed and never get up again. Or maybe I should just make a pot of coffee and pretend everything is normal. Just for today, just for this morning, just for this minute, I want to make believe that everything really is okay and Marvin will come through the door any second, announcing, "Dorrie, I'm back," clutching a crumpled paper bag full of honey-glazed Dunkin Donuts which he knows I can never resist.

If only.

I let out my trademark sigh, and listen to the sounds of the kitchen: the hum of the toaster oven, the gurgle of the coffee maker, the clank of plates, glasses, and silverware as I place them on the glass top of the table. Sounds I've heard a million times before. Sounds that used to be comforting, just like the smells that are now filling the kitchen: the freshly brewed French vanilla coffee and the almost-but-not-quite burnt bagels, which is just the way Marvin likes them. Liked them. Used to like them. Will never like them again.

Tiferet

Okay, I say, or I think I say. I know I moved my lips but I didn't hear any sound come out.

I lean my now-bony tuchus against the counter and close my eyes as if doing so could make all this go away. The toaster oven dings, its tinny jarring sound making me hop to before the bagels really burn. I slide them out of the toaster oven, arrange them in a little straw basket, and bring them to the table. Then I take two cups out of the cabinet, wincing at the sight of the "World's Greatest Dad" mug that Rhonda bought Marvin one year for Father's Day—something else I might as well throw away—and fill them with coffee. Then I set one cup at my place and one in front of Burt.

"Thanks, Mrs. B.," Burt says. He waits as he always does, like a puppy at attention who dares not make a move without his master's command. I want to deliver my line, "Help yourself, Burt," but I can't push the words out of my mouth. This is just wrong. I shouldn't be sharing breakfast with my cleaning guy. I should be sharing breakfast with my guy-guy. My husband. My Marvin.

It's all too much, I think as I grip the edge of the table to steady myself. *It's okay,* I remind myself. *Go sit down.* But instead of collapsing onto my own chair, my feet bring me around to the other side of the table where I fall onto Burt's lap, bury my face into that tender spot where a man's neck meets his shoulder, bunch a small corner of his spotless white tee shirt into my fist as if it were a baby blanket, and finally allow myself to weep.

NONFICTION

The Boy at the Bus Stop

William Kenower

I was driving home one afternoon when I spotted a teenage boy sitting on the curb on the road at a bus stop. His head was down, and he was leaning forward with his elbows resting on his knees. The street was busy that afternoon, and car after car rolled by, but he did not lift his head.

While I didn't know this boy, I recognized much about him. First, he reminded me of the boys I avoided when I was young. I was not a fighter, though I often imagined being armed with the quietly lethal powers of David Carradine's character in the 70's television show *Kung Fu*. To be able to get about the world fearlessly, knowing that if the wicked violence of the world should visit me I could escape not merely unharmed but—with a righteous, spiritually centered kick and jab—having made the world a slightly safer place by felling one of its many, many villains. But I was just not a fighter. I learned early that I had no desire to hurt anyone, even someone who looked like a bad guy. You have to get close to someone to hit them, and the closer I got to anyone the less villainous they seemed.

Which is why I avoided certain boys. They looked like they were coiled and ready to strike at all times, and I did not trust that if we crossed paths they would not strike out at me. Except it really wasn't the boys I didn't trust, but myself. Just as there were lion tamers who could stand safely with animals built by nature to kill with one bite or cowboys who could soothe a wild horse, so too I sensed there was a way to be with these boys without igniting that smoldering hostility—but I did not know that way. So I avoided them, wavering between feeling shame for what seemed like fear in me, and hatred for what seemed like senseless antagonism in them.

But I recognized something else in the boy at the bus stop. Even from my car I could see that his attention was entirely with his thoughts. He was not staring at his shoe tops; he was not considering some crack in the road. He had gone, as I often have, within himself, to that interior kingdom of memory and imagination, but also of grievances and dreams, and of inspiration and dread. I know all too well that this kingdom can be as treacherous as it is life giving. I also know that whatever current landscape it offers, it is possible to disappear entirely into that kingdom, to see only my own castles and dragons, while the world of ranch houses and pickup trucks continues to hum all about me.

Tiferet

All this occurred in one glance as the traffic slowed to a halt. I tapped my wheel, still considering the boy at the bus stop. He seemed unhappy, and I found myself thinking about how easy it is to deaden your own spirits, but how challenging it can be to lift someone else's. As I was tapping and thinking, the car in front of me decided to make a break for it. It was only a two-lane road, however, and because there was oncoming traffic in the other lane, he had to pass on the right. He pulled out, gunning his engine to gain a little speed. There was enough room in the road for the stalled cars, the passing car, and the boy's feet—but only just. As the car roared past the bus stop, the boy looked up with a start, pulled from his thoughts by his sudden proximity to the mass of noise and power and that is a moving car. For an instant he looked stunned and innocent: a boy awakened violently from a dream to a world that had become dangerous while he slept. And then he changed.

Up came the middle finger, and then his fist, and then he was shouting at the car as it drove away. He shouted and shook his first with what seemed like the same familiar body memory with which a pugilist throws a punch. I had cursed like that a handful of times in my life, each time hoping something would be released, and each time learning that there was more to be released after the cursing than before. I always felt like a stranger to myself when I did it, but a stranger I could learn to know if I practiced.

As the traffic started up again, the boy's rant ended as naturally as a sentence. In the next moment my car had pulled even with him. He was back to leaning on his knees, but staring ahead now, blinking dully. I wanted to let my eyes linger on him, to study him like an animal found the wild, but I knew how you could feel someone's eyes on you even through the windows of a nearby car, and I did not think he would read a stranger's stare as friendly.

The traffic flowed forward and I thought how interesting it is that we can know when someone is looking at us. It defies a certain kind of physical logic. I'm in my car and he's on the curb. We're separate. Except, if you want to stay safe in this world, you quickly learn that the opposite is true, and that's where it gets a little confusing. It is so easy, so automatic and reflexive, to see how we are different; it takes concentration to remember how we are not, to remember that every villain is caught in a dream into which they retreated, hoping to stay safe from a world they had forgotten how to trust.

NONFICTION

What is so Great About Being Grateful?

RJ Jeffreys

Throughout my early childhood, my family and I would drive 100 miles east across the state of Massachusetts to visit my grandparents. They lived in an ample, well-maintained Victorian style home in a placid suburb just north of Boston.

As the adults settled in to catch up on family news; I would dash into the living room and jump into a large wingback armchair. It sat next to a wide picture window and was my favorite chair.

My Nana Addie always followed closely behind to watch me perform my circus leap into that seat. She would then take my little hands into hers, pull me up and out of the chair, and gently draw me back into it and onto her lap. I would nestle as deeply as I could into that comforting place. And, in my young imagination, I believed that my Nana and that overstuffed chair were always there waiting patiently just for me.

It was there I would bombard my infinitely patient Nana with a million questions about life and the world, which were still so fresh to me. Within those queries was a singular thought of how peaceful and serene she always appeared. Later in life, as I became aware of how extremely arduous her life had been, I admired her perpetual positivity even more.

Nana Addie had borne twelve children. One of them had died during childbirth and another had severe learning disabilities. My Grandfather was a dictatorial and serious sort, who played the role of absolute patriarch in their home. That was another heavy burden she unfalteringly carried every day, and always without even a whisper of complaint. Addie lived each day of her life with unfaltering grace, dignity, and an overflowing of unconditional love for everyone.

My parents divorced when I was twelve, and my mother, two brothers, and I moved back east and into my Grandfather's house. I had grown too large to fit into Nana Addie's comforting lap, but we still had many wonderful talks, albeit in our own separate chairs.

I was very curious about the distinct characterological contrasts between my Grandparents. That eventually prompted me ask, "Nana Addie, how are you always so cheerful and at peace?"

(Here's where the true meaning of gratitude enters the picture).

In her infinitely calm manner, Addie replied, "I know that my life has not been an easy one. And I do get very tired at times. But what I realised many years ago was that as long as I was truly grateful for what I had—like having all my wonderful children and grandchildren around me—I would never fret about what I didn't have. And I would never feel jealous or envious of what anyone else had that I did not. And, right at this moment, I'm most grateful to be talking with you, my angel!"

Nana Addie's indelible answer has been instrumental in sustaining me through all the difficult times in my own life. And has helped me to empathize and appreciate that everyone who faces their own life's shortcomings can remain grateful for what they still have.

When I was seventeen, and Nana Addie had just turned seventy; she was rushed by ambulance to our local hospital and quickly admitted. The grave diagnosis of her condition was acute kidney failure. I sped to be by her side there. And with my legs feeling like two granite columns, I entered her private room and took her delicate hands gently in mine.

For the very first time in my life, I witnessed deep distress on my Grandmother's now pallid face. I asked her in quavering tones how she was feeling. She could only reply in pleading whispers, "Please, take me home. I don't want to stay here." Knowing her very poor prognosis, I suddenly felt a crushing fear as my legs turned to powder.

My vigil was abruptly interrupted by a light knock on the hospital room door. A nurse entered and glanced at Nana Addie's hands enfolded in mine. She smiled at us and asked, "Are you Jeffrey?"

I replied, "Yes".

"Your Grandmother has been asking us to call you, ever since we admitted her. And I can see she's very happy you're with her now. We're transferring her to the ICU, but you can stay five more minutes. And, then you can come back in about two hours and go to the ICU unit to see her."

I thanked the nurse, and in the few minutes I had left did my best to reassure my Nana. I promised that I absolutely would come back to take her home with me.

Leaving my car in the hospital lot, I walked the mile and a half back to my house in the hope it would help to ease my fear. I resolved to keep my promise to Nana Addie.

My mother was seated on our front porch when I arrived home. I could see that she was crying. She spoke to me in broken breaths, "The hospital called about a half an hour ago, and they said your Nana passed away".

In utter disbelief, all I could blurt out was, "Why?!"

I believe we all do the best we can in coping with the profound losses that press on our hearts throughout life. For me, after that darkest day, I stopped asking, "Why?" Instead, I remember Nana Addie's sagacious words, and that long ago I blissfully sat nestled in unconditional love and on her most comforting lap. And, with that I always do answer, "What is so great about being grateful?" for myself.

I am certain that if you look deeply inside of your own selves today, you will find something to be truly grateful about, too.

Marcia Krause Bilyik   IRKUTSKAYA YEPARKHIYA

POETRY

Nietzsche's Ghazal

Arthur Solway

It comes to you again, the question of being human.
You've pondered the expression to be human,

all too human, but what does it mean?
Lamenting the so-called human

condition, we move through disquieting days,
scrolling images of the inhumane—

how a history of humankind isn't easily mended.
At the end of what we've called humanity

what can you tell us? Tell us it will be fine,
it'll be OK. Tell us we're only human.

NONFICTION

Hope is a Voice

Lisa Romeo

Late at night, fighting fear-fueled insomnia, herb tea is useless. I look to old movies and not-so-old movies—hoping, for something.

That's where I find the voice, the one with the all-knowing, all-kind, godlike benevolence. The voice that calms, carries me back to hope.

I'm talking about Morgan Freeman. About the final minutes of *The Shawshank Redemption*.

About the way his character lives *with* hope, after living without hope, because his friend Andy advised, "Hope is a good thing. Maybe the best of things." When I try to explain those last film moments, I don't tell it right. I'm still trying to hope the way Red, paroled murderer turned mellowed old man, hopes, while making his wistful, yearning way to Andy:

"I hope to see my friend and shake his hand. I hope the Pacific is as blue as it has been in my dreams. I hope."

My words don't sing as lyrically as in Freeman's mouth, on film against endless blue sea, welcoming shore. But I find the movie often, so I'm getting closer. I close my eyes. I picture Shepard Fairey's *Hope* silhouette, that other face that calmed, carried me, carried us all.

I hope.

Conny Jasper   SPRING BUDS

POETRY

Life Still

Jane Ebihara

alone
on this Pennsylvania hillside
I watch layers of mountain and sky share
motionless waves of greens and blues
like some vast unreachable ocean

still life with song
sonorous invitations and responses
tossed tree to tree

the birds
in search of…
rejoicing in…
yearning for…

how many languages do they speak
or is it only one   they
so much better at brotherhood
than we

see how that Finch has no fear
of the Phoebe's call

she has her own voice

you're gone ten months now
and I am a little less lost each day

Tiferet

if I believed in heaven
I would wish you here

on this hillside
with this music
in this perfect
still
life

NONFICTION

Finding God in My Gi

Ilona Fried

Most of my life, I avoided white clothing. White magnetizes spills and stains. It requires vigilance and effort to keep it pristine. Even after I, a stubborn outsider, reluctantly joined a synagogue following my father's unexpected passing to fill the enormous void he left behind, I didn't wear white on Yom Kippur like many congregants. Instead, I put on an ivory long sleeve blouse and a coordinated faux suede skirt I'd found at a local shop. The almost-but-not-quite white kept me a few subtle shades away from conformity. Perhaps from God, too, even though Yom Kippur had long been the highlight of my religious experience. The fasting, the suspension of bathing and grooming, and the intensity of daylong prayer left me feeling more invigorated and renewed than any activity the secular world had on offer. I couldn't imagine my life without the Day of Atonement. Yet despite my willingness to observe this holiday more wholeheartedly and sincerely than any other, I couldn't bring myself to get a white outfit. I had the money, but perhaps I couldn't buy into Judaism one hundred percent. Much of the time, my birth religion felt like a complex, fussy garment that pinched when I tried to move and never felt just right.

Nine years after I last paid membership dues to a synagogue, and a few years since I donated that ivory blouse and skirt to Goodwill, I now wear a white *gi* three times a week at the Aikido dojo where I train. I relate to the *gi* not as sporting attire but as a ritual garment like the *kittel*, a white linen robe donned by men during Yom Kippur. The *kittel* also serves as a burial shroud and is worn as a reminder that the holiest day of the year is also a rehearsal of the end of life, a chance to purify oneself before God. In its simplicity and absence of pockets, so that nothing can accompany the deceased, the *kittel* assures equality in death, which reduces us all to bones. If am not careful, I can easily become blinded by appearance, achievements, and power, and forget that all humans are ultimately vulnerable, relying on skeletons to support us as we navigate in the gravitational field. Aikido reminds me that I have a skeleton and teaches me how to use it well, in service of life.

At the dojo, as I change out of my street clothes and put on loose cotton pants as bright as new snow, I think about Yom Kippur and the holiday's life and death intensity. I think of the parts of my history and of myself that I need to release

73

and grieve so that I can move forward and feel fully alive, even if that vitality takes an unfamiliar form or takes me to unexpected places. I think of Jewish men, and now women, who in preparation for morning prayers wrap the leather straps of *tefillin* around their left arms and foreheads in a prescribed manner. I never felt called to wear phylacteries, but I connect with the need for ritual to invite a state change. Before leaving the dressing room, I make sure that the left lapel of my jacket overlaps the right, in keeping with Japanese tradition, and that I have tied the belt properly. To step into my *gi* is to step away from contemporary society, to step out of my persona, to step into humility, and step before the unknown. To remove my street clothes, chosen to flatter me, and put on a loose fitting uniform worn by millions across the centuries and around the globe is to choose the life-giving practice of Aikido rather than the slow death of remaining in my comfort zone, a deeply etched groove which often keeps me stuck in my head and out of the arena. Before class begins, as if readying myself for a *mikveh*, a ritual immersion, I trim my nails and remove my jewelry, a silver ring I made years before, so as not to injure myself or another when plunging into the energetic practice of "the way of harmonious spirit" or "the way of unifying life energy," two translations of Aikido. Its founder, Morihei Ueshiba, referred to it as "The Art of Peace."

A hush descends upon the dojo before class starts. The pale green tatami mats squeak gently as students move across them to kneel in a line. Cars and buses thrum outside, but the interior silence comes as a relief, a chance to regroup and focus my mind. The *sensei* (teacher) waits to the side before kneeling in front of the group, his back to us. We all bow to the front of the room and when the *sensei* turns to face us, the students bow to him. Before beginning a round of practice, we face our partners and bow to them. We bow again and again. Sometimes I am dizzied by the sheer amount of bowing, by the frequency with which we drop to our knees. I bow to people I might not acknowledge and who might not give me a second glance if we were to pass each other on the street or at a supermarket. At the dojo we can't always pick and choose who our partners will be.

As Ueshiba said, "Always practice the Art of Peace in a vibrant and joyful manner." To do so means constantly navigating the ever-shifting obstacle course created by my ego, which has erected numerous barriers and hurdles to participation and connection. There is a man whose prickly stubble and pointy teeth I'd rather not gaze at, which means I must rapidly redirect my attention beyond the superficial so I can find harmony, the essence of the practice. He has earned at least one black belt, and when he gives me advice in a heavy Boston accent which my ears want to close against, I must re-calibrate my reaction, listen, and thank him. There are the men dripping with sweat, their skin so slick I can barely hang on when it's my turn to attack and grab their wrist. I must remain connected until they throw me, rather than slip away prematurely, even when my squeamish self wants to interrupt the flow and dry my hands. At almost every moment my mind manufactures an objection or provides an excuse to bow off the mat. Being attacked comes as a relief: it swiftly silences the mind's chatter and brings me into the moment. I spring into action.

* * *

In the Book of Genesis, Jacob wrestles with either an angel or God himself, who strikes Jacob in the thigh during a night-long sparring match. In persisting, Jacob is renamed Israel, "because you have struggled with the divine and with men, and you have prevailed." The encounter leaves Jacob with a limp. The story is etched in my memory. I have often longed for a similar, mysterious, non-verbal encounter, a transmission of some kind that would permanently free me from fear and self-consciousness and leave me transformed; perhaps not with a different name, but with a new lease on life. As a girl and younger woman, I occasionally tussled with my brothers or boyfriends. There is something primal and purifying in grappling with another human, limb to limb, torso to torso, rather than engaging in a verbal sparring match, no matter how good-natured. At times the body in motion can express the truth better than words.

* * *

When I began practicing Aikido I had the impulse to wrestle my partners, to wield my strength and apply force rather than use finesse and the laws of physics to bring them to the floor. The *sensei* intervened.

"It's not wrestling," he said. "It's more like a dance. You're flowing together."

The first time I attacked my teacher, he took my balance and spiraled me to the ground so swiftly and adeptly that I laughed from the profound pleasure of the surprise. It was as if his energy and mine had temporarily joined to form the swirling strands of a double helix, the source of life itself, injecting me with a surge of vitality. I jumped up to repeat the experience, one that rivaled the thrill of hiking wilderness trails and tall peaks, something I did for more than a decade in search of connection to the divine.

To blend with an attacker is counter-intuitive and confounding. It demands training to rewire primitive fight-flight-freeze reflexes into a relaxed yet alert flow state. Learning to apply the appropriate amount of pressure for partners of different shapes, sizes, and skill levels is an art form. The more I practice, the more I become aware of the myriad, if not endless, subtleties, and the degree of precision that make Aikido's entrancing, circular, fluid movements possible. To "go with the flow" is no simple matter, either on or off the mat. Still, I continue to wrestle, not with fellow students, but against ingrained habits of mind and the ghosts of my former selves. I wrestle with the voice that says Aikido and the sixty-minute round trip commute to the dojo take time away from writing and the life of the mind. This voice elevates the cerebral and the contemplative over the physical, forgetting that mind and body are one, and that if I don't properly care for my body, I could quickly compromise my mind. I grapple with an ancestral voice that kvetches that I should remain in my own cultural lane rather than learning an obscure body art with samurai influences. It tells me that Aikido is for "other people," even though anyone, regardless of fitness level or experience, can learn Aikido. I argue with a voice that tells me I am too old to be doing this. Since I can't practice as vigorously as a twenty-five-year-old, why bother?

I must prevail against these voices or risk remaining stiff and frozen in both body and mind out of a false sense of superiority, inferiority, or otherness. I wrestle the ghosts to the periphery of my consciousness so I can tuck my head, surrender to gravity and momentum, and roll forwards and backwards on the dojo's thick mats. To tumble quickly along the ground astonishes and delights me as if I were a child discovering how to move for the first time even though I recently turned fifty. If I were to cling to my ego identity—a complex if not calcified web of beliefs that even the intense chanting of ancient Jewish prayers couldn't always crack apart so my spirit could breathe—I would not experience the healing power of connecting to another, allowing life energy, or *ki*, to circulate through both of us as our skeletons spiral, bend, and twist together. If I entertained the doubts, I would not spend hours each week refining my movements and inscribing my nervous system with fresh, life-giving habits, writing an invisible book of health and, hopefully, longevity.

Some progressive rabbis, trying to soften the traditional and dramatic narrative of Yom Kippur, when God determines who will live another year and who will die, have reframed it as the Day of At-One-Ment. They emphasize congruence more than repentance and remind people that wholeness is a form of holiness. Such wholeness, which I've experienced around animals and in nature, had eluded me around people until I began practicing Aikido. Something alchemical happens when I have thrown myself into the action, been thrown onto the mat, and thrown others, too. The body-on-body, bone-to-bone intimacy empties me of self, yet leaves me, paradoxically, whole. I feel kindness and at times affection towards my partners, even the slick and sweaty ones, even the people who express impatience as I repeatedly fumble my way through an unfamiliar maneuver, even the man with the heavy Boston accent. The deep satisfaction of practicing temporarily blurs what had been thickly and distinctly drawn lines between myself and other. I wondered if that experience of harmony would quickly fade once the novelty wore off. When it didn't, I began to read books about Aikido. In *The Art of Peace,* a pocket-sized compilation of Ueshiba's teachings translated by John Stevens, it says: "The Art of Peace is a form of prayer that generates light and heat. Forget about your little self, detach yourself from objects, and you will radiate light and warmth."

No one I've met at the dojo has used the word prayer, but that is what Aikido is for me. Maybe it is for them, too, but that doesn't matter. During practice, we speak only if necessary. Otherwise, we move wordlessly, the silence punctuated by loud slaps on the mat when the attacker hits the ground. During a full, fast-paced class, the series of slaps mimics the boom-boom-boom of firecrackers. It's a sound I've come to welcome rather than recoil against. I think of it as the sacred sound of egos disintegrating or combusting so the spirit can be polished. To my surprise, I've discovered that I don't mind the frequent washing the white *gi* requires. I prefer to practice in freshly cleaned clothing, to honor myself and my partners as we move in what still feels like mysterious ways on this exhilarating and deeply humbling spiritual path.

POETRY

A Suite for Gandhi

Lynn Domina

i.
Later, I will follow
his footprints their last
hundred meters toward the stone marker
where the eager crowd waited
and later

I will witness
chrysanthemums glowing
where his son
ignited his pyre

but now I only
watch the film, thinking
no as the beautiful
thin man emerges
to greet
his assassin.

ii.
Gandhi, Gandhi-ji,
I have learned so little.

iii.
As his body
crumples, I recall the scene
when he was tossed off
the South African train, tumbling
in dust, his British suit heavy with heat.

iv.
I have begun to learn
how to refuse
cooperation with those powers
craving my oppression,
but I have only begun to learn
how to convert
my rage into peace.

v.
Standing at the foot
of his narrow bed, I saw
his spindle, his glasses, a small lamp.
Everything I need
to know resides
in the space of that sparse room
and in his footprints leading
from there along the path
to the crowd.

vi.
I have said peace
be upon you.
I have recited
shanti, shanti, shanti
oh beautiful man.

NONFICTION

How to Become a Ghost

Laraine Herring

Gentle Reader,

I don't want to surprise you. I want to make this easy for you so it doesn't sneak up on you and leave you defenseless. You think it can't happen to you because of whatever perceived advantages you thought you had. You thought you were special, but you're just like everyone else, thinking your hold on yourself was unbreakable. Maybe it ultimately is, but even the stealthiest of winter animals go into hiding.

Please put down your teacup.

Do you remember reading the old fashioned books that called you gentle from the moment you opened the cover? The ones that believed in your compassion and empathy as a reader, your willingness to tumble heart-first into the story? The ones that didn't start off with a shout, a call to action, or a hunted woman needing saving? The ones that let you slip and slide slowly into a story before beginning *in medias res*?

(Really, Freytag, the story starts long before the action and inciting event, and if you had the patience to follow its tracks, you might be able to avert the gunfight, the ejaculation at the top of the pyramid, but I know, I know. Today's readers are not gentle. They do not have that patience. Too many things tweeting for their time. Get in. Get out. That's the story.)

But maybe that's why we never recognize the stories when they're happening to us. We forget there's a slow simmer before the boil. We forget there is always time to turn the kettle off. But what would be the fun in that? After all, Freytag, your special effects budget is equal to the GDP of Ecuador. Mustn't waste a chance to waste.

Let's return, Gentle Reader, to this essay. You might have thought this was a rollicking ghost story á la Shirley Jackson, or maybe a darker one, like Joe Hill's work. But this isn't that. If the spook comes to you at all, it will be when you find yourself in the mirror of the story.

Drop a lump of sugar in that tea, if you must, to sweeten the taste.

Touch up your lipstick to make sure you reflect in the smoky glass.

Follow closely.

Watch for the story that started long before the directions.
Never mistake the moment of crisis for the moment of change.
The moment of change occurs much, much earlier.

And do take notes. There will be no exam, but it will nonetheless be tested.

<Ms. Albright, I'm sorry for the lack of parallelism in the outline. Yes, I do know better. But the steps are anything but parallel. I know this will cost me points. I'd rather lose points than tell the wrong story.>

How to Become a Ghost

1) Experience a recent trauma that begins the loosening of your skin from your bones.

    1a) Don't notice that your skin has been loosened from your bones. Enjoy the pleasure of dropping a pants size without trying. Your new book, *The Grief Diet*, will be a bestseller. Equate the loosening of your flesh with success and progress. You're becoming the thin girl inside the fat body your grandmother always said was there. *Such a pretty face.*

    1b) Try not to think of your father six feet under in the plot by the oleander bushes, his skin loosening from his bones.

2) Notice that when moving through the world as a fat woman, you were invisible. As a thin woman, you are noticed, but not for your brain or your writing or your compassion. You're noticed for your boobs and your butt, and you have no tools for this attention. You were the fat girl long before you became the fat woman. The thin woman is helpless, unarmed without layers of squishy flesh. You are beautiful in your hunger. Everyone says so.

    2a) When the suave Italian man notices you, the fat woman who now lives inside the thin woman was repulsed. But the thin woman, who could never wear the tight jeans and the sleeveless top she's now sporting, dances over to him and smiles.

    2b) In the cold dark of his coffin, your father tries to hold onto his finger flesh long enough to call you on the phone. Long enough to tell you to stop. But he can't find the wires underground. The mouthpiece is missing.

Tiferet

3) Agree to go out with the suave Italian that you feel drawn to and repulsed by. Don't realize that what you want most of all is not to feel anything.

    3a) When he kisses you, it shimmies all the way to your toes and you decide it must be love.

    3b) Your father's skeleton fingers try to push at the lid of the casket, try to get back to you, but you dance in too-tight jeans and you play house with the Italian and you can't hear the bony fingers knocking at your door.

4) Move away from your family and move in with the Italian. You cannot bear to be alone, but you think you have grown up and started living. You aren't wise enough to know that death and life embody the same skin—that with each new cell you generate, another one disappears.

    4a) When you wind up paying for everything—the rent, the food, the gas—you decide you are a modern woman. You don't believe you are being played.

    4b) Your father remembers he told you to never leave the house without twenty dollars. He is angry that he didn't live long enough to tell you that there were also men who would stay with you just because you had twenty dollars.

5) Be excited that you and the Italian enjoyed writing and think that you will be able to share this activity and support each other in it.

    5a) Watch him throw a tantrum in your intro to fiction class when your work was received better than his. Listen to him tell you it was your fault. You were trying to humiliate him. You have no experience to compare this to. Maybe you did do it on purpose. Did you write too well to overshadow him? It will be decades before you learn the words:

    Projection.
    Gaslighting.
    Bullshit.

    5b) The mouthpiece is unattached to the telephone and it hangs upside down in your father's skeleton fingers like a bat. Or a regret.

6) Stop writing.*

    * You were never that good anyway, and it isn't worth the trouble. His rage scares you, so you meet it with silence. With complacence.

With complicity. You don't notice your own rage bubbling in the cauldron of your empty belly.

6a) This isn't what you imagined your twenties to be like. This isn't what college had promised. But you cannot leave him now. You know what it feels like to be left and you will never do that to another person.

6b) "I didn't leave you," says your father, but there is no dial tone, no receiver, no plump skin at the cheeks, no bobbing Adam's apple at the throat. He is sinking, but he can't let go of the mouthpiece. There was so much more he had left to say.

7) Begin to steal from the movie theatre where you work. Small bills. Never too much. You're the manager, so you can write the difference off in damaged merchandise—a tangled Red Vine here, a molded hot dog there. Write off the food. It isn't necessary. Then you can pay for the things he wants—the nice dinners, the nice clothes. Then you can avoid the conflict and the fight.

7a) The Italian is upset that you work so much and is convinced you're having an affair. Your lack of desire for him must mean you are engaged with another.

7b) "I didn't have enough time to tell you everything I wanted you to know," your father thinks he speaks, but the mouthpiece is impotent and he no longer has a tongue. He has grown accustomed to the dark and has made friends with the worms that have taken his liver. There is beauty in their hunger.

8) Have an affair with your first love, whom you run into at the movie theatre where you work (so the Italian can have nice dinners, nice clothes). Your first love met your father years ago and you cannot resist that connection, that chance to keep your father alive. Plus. Sex without the promise of violence is nice. When you lie next to your first love you can sleep. You begin to eat, two meals a day now, and the Italian calls you fat, your breasts banana tits, your ass Jell-O.

8a) You're a modern woman now. Going to college. Working. Having an affair and keeping your own apartment. Twenty is so very old. You will never be this old again.

8b) Your father was forty-six when he died and he finds that terribly young. He hadn't yet wrinkled and puckered. He simply stopped after years of almost-stopping, years of heart attacks followed by the inevitable, unforgivable return of the polio that had crippled him when he was seven.

He could not fight that again. It was time to dissolve. But under the earth with his worms and his limp leg and limp mouthpiece, he couldn't leave the living dirt.

9) Duck when he throws the butcher knife at your head. "If I wanted to hit you I would have," he says and takes your car keys and subsequently your car and leaves you alone in the apartment you are paying for. You make scrambled eggs and eat them without chewing so you won't change your mind.

    9a) Put away all the dishes. Make the bed and clean the bathroom. Wash his clothes with yours in the communal laundry. Feel the urge to protect your skinny jeans from touching his as they tumble in the heat.

    9b) The worms haven't come for his lungs yet and he has one last breath in him—the exhale he'd been holding onto because you were there in the beeping yellow room on the morning he died and he couldn't release it because that would mean he would leave you and your mother and your sister and he was so very tired but he couldn't go so he held and the worms didn't understand how his lungs were pink and pulsing while all around the skeleton the flesh fell in silent chunks.

    Still.

    Mad respect from the worms.

10) Consciously eliminate all your options for escape. You cannot tell anyone what it has been like with the Italian. You have become one of the women you have always pitied—the one who stayed. Suddenly, your heart expands with compassion as you realize that staying or going is not a black and white decision. It is not about having resources or options or places to go. It is about believing you deserve to have those options. You left your grieving family. You left your friends. You wanted to dissolve into the Italian and another life and you have achieved that. You always achieve what you put in motion, but you are not always wise enough to discern what you've started.

    10a) The Italian quits his job at Sizzler after just a few weeks because it is beneath him. He is meant to be an attorney. He is meant to be wealthy. You are still cleaning up soda and popcorn from the floors of the movie theatres and you're now managing to pocket $200 a week in small bills so he can eat like he's rich.

    10b) The exhale is pressing up against the edges of his lungs and he knows he will have to release it or he will burst inside the coffin. The mouthpiece is touching the gape of his nose cavity and he thinks he might be able to make a sound. The breath is climbing up his esophagus. There is no more time.

11) Eighteen months after your father died, you come home after class (no more writing classes, just literature classes, the words of others) to the apartment you are paying for so the Italian feels rich, and there is a message on your answering machine from him. "Sugar," your father says. "Get out." Beep.

(Gentle Reader: this is the part of the essay that is not a metaphor. Drink your tea. Feel it hot in your throat. Feel it coat your breath with steam. Look around your room. Is there a shiver beneath your yellow wallpaper? A silver shimmer at the window?)

11a) You don't leave then, but now you know you will.

11b) There is no more breath and your father is exhausted and his lungs are collapsing like ellipses at the ends of paragraphs and he thinks he can go now but...

12) You load up your car in the dark and you leave for an undisclosed location. You can walk away from it all except ...

you reach for his voice:

Sugar.

Sugar.

Sugar.

...and catch it in a jar like a firefly. You tighten the lid and set it on the dashboard of your orange AMC Spirit. Your own bones rattle in your loose skin; the moon is a thin sheath, its cool blue light unable to illuminate either of you, specters now, conspiring in shared darkness and running out of breath.

POETRY

Grave Blanket

Michelle Ortega

This is part of Christmas now: a pine spray, boxwood and red ribbon—a blanket for your grave.

Are you cold? I am drenched, chilled to the bone on this dark noon. No shield from the sting of winter rain in my hair, on my skin, through the soles of my sneakers. I place a small snowflake-light on the soggy boughs and watch the LED shift from red to green to blue, oddly festive, and wonder how long the battery will last.

Joy and grief are indistinguishable. You are free and strong and part of everything lovely:

> I shiver —
> and breathe

FICTION

Three Days

Dheepa R. Maturi

Day One

When Meena's husband died, she was told that his soul would try very hard to hold onto its body, that it would linger and poke and push its way into the world of matter unless they took the *appropriate steps*, steps laid out thousands of years ago and followed ever since. *Would a lingering soul be so bad?* she wondered.

But the mourning mechanism pushed forward relentlessly, and Meena soon found herself surrounded by a downcast crowd, Sanskrit phrases intoning from the priest steadily and methodically in the background. The crematorium had been readied by a calm and kind funeral director, now familiar with Indian ceremonies, no longer puzzled by the required and assorted customs.

She found that her autonomic brain was able to answer questions and respond to fellow mourners appropriately, so she allowed her mind to remain in neutral, absorbing the cadences around her. The solicitous questions from her devastated mother, the sympathetic whispers from the crowd, the calm directives of the funeral director — all washed through her as she sat with strange equanimity, hands folded in her lap.

She'd been so angry with Vishal last week about his unwillingness to share housework, even to pick up his socks, but now of course she only thought about the open smile that charmed even the grouchy neighbors and the clever hands that fixed the erratic furnace in their ancient house.

Meena shifted her body and leaned on her mother's shoulder, letting her head droop, making those around her think that she was overcome by emotion. Meena was simply tired, worn through by the onslaught of arrangements required — hospital, family, funeral director, lawyer.

The Sanskrit pulsed on and on, asking Vishal's soul to depart, imploring it to move on peacefully, to bother no more about the world of the living. A tiny oil lamp, small enough to fit in her palm, had been lit and now sat on the mantle of the artificial fireplace next to her. The lamp would need to be watched continuously, kept fed and lit, and then, after three days, allowed to burn out. Her mother had explained this responsibility to her tearfully before the funeral began.

She closed her eyes and felt herself throb along with the sounds.

"Meena?" A voice seemed to pipe directly into her mind.

She started, but did not lift her head, did not trust herself, did not trust her mind.

The voice sounded distant, but its timbre was familiar. "Meena!"

"Vishal?" Her voice barely emerged from her lips.

Every instinct pushed her to open her eyes, to shake her head and disregard the nonsense her brain was creating, but her heart had swollen wide and would not dismiss the possibility.

"Vishal?" she croaked, louder this time.

Her mother looked at her, troubled.

The voice returned, distorted, and she could not understand it. "Meena - need - need..."

She jolted up, suddenly aware that the chanting had ceased, realizing that Vishal's body would now be carried to the crematorium. Who had started screaming? Shocked, Meena realized the sounds were emerging from her, from the gut of her gut, startling the crowd who had witnessed her calm demeanor throughout the ceremony. She launched her body onto Vishal's, pulling it close, holding it away from the purposeful men who advanced upon him. Meena felt the tug of her mother behind her, urgent whispers against her ear, arms encircling her waist, dragging her away from the body, from Vishal, from her former life.

She strained against the people around her, against the disturbed murmurs, until her body gave in. Propelled none-too-gently into a large armchair, she crouched over her knees, shaking.

Day Two

Meena awoke slowly, as though pushing through a haze, the objects around her coming into focus only one at a time. She tried to delay the moment when comprehension would flood her mind, tried to linger in the dream space, the space of No Knowledge, as long as she could. Then her stomach heaved and released the events of the past week. Meena threw her arm across her eyes to avert the light — no one had thought to draw the blinds. The clock was missing from her night stand; in its place was an empty glass and a bottle of pills. She squeezed her eyes closed. Why would someone leave that bottle so close to her?

And what had gotten into her yesterday, hearing Vishal's voice, losing all control of herself, screaming in front of a room full of people? She was a practical person, logical and reasonable, and now she felt ashamed. Her throat tightened. She could not move.

After a few minutes, Meena gathered her strength and turned slowly to her side. Squinting one eye open, she saw her mother sleeping on the floor on an air mattress. Poor Mom, she looked older than usual, crumpled by her daughter's grief, but holding herself together for Meena's sake. On the dresser above the sleeping form was the oil lamp, burning brightly — her mother must have tended it through the night on Meena's behalf. She spotted the bedside alarm clock on the floor.

Meena shut her eyes again. *Breathe, breathe, breathe.* When that became too difficult, Meena decided to concentrate only on her inhalations, making them as wide and long as possible till her body had no choice but to exhale. *Inhale. Inhale. Inhale.* Panic crept close by.

"Meena!" The voice pressed gently into her head. Her eyelids flew open. Had she only imagined the crematorium? Her body froze while the garbling continued, and she strained, willed her brain to comprehend the sounds. After minutes of terrible tension, Meena almost shouted in frustration, but suddenly, the oil lamp on the dresser caught her eye. Meena tiptoed around her mother and made her way toward it.

"I need to tell you, Meena." Vishal's voice, at last, sounded clear in her head.

Meena could not prevent a sob from escaping, and her mother stirred, eyelids fluttering open. "Meena! Are you okay?" Concerned, she struggled to sit up.

Meena feared that Vishal's voice would drain away again. She knew now that his presence was tied to the lamp, but only tenuously.

"Mom," croaked Meena, "I could really use some water."

Meena's mother rose quickly, anxious to help, to do something that was needed. When the older woman exited, Meena turned quickly back to the lamp.

"Vishal! I'm so sorry. I'm sorry for everything."

"Don't worry, darling. Darling Meena."

"Vishal, where are you? Are you in this room? Are you here with me?"

There was a pause. "Meena, I don't know — I have to leave, but I need to..."

"Vishal! I'm so sorry about last week. I'm so sorry for everything, and I think I'm going crazy."

"Meena, I need to tell you..."

Meena heard the door open, and turned to find her mother eyeing her strangely.

Vishal was gone.

Tiferet

Meena remained in bed that day, tending the lamp and waiting, asking to be left alone when anyone inquired after her. Lying on her side, propped up by pillows, she watched the faint line of black smoke rise from the semicircle of brass as hours slipped by. Vishal did not return.

Day Three

Time began to feel liquid, illusory to Meena as she moved in and out of consciousness and sleep, dizzy and nauseated, checking the lamp, waiting. Her memories, kept consciously at bay till now, loosened and surfaced as exhaustion seeped into her cells.

She and Vishal had met and dated in college, though this had been an unexpected turn of events for Meena, who planned to focus entirely on her studies. She and her parents had scratched out an existence in New York studio apartments, managing family life in dusty and cramped quarters. Her father had left a lucrative position in India, wanting more education and opportunity for his only child — a little girl, and therefore at a disadvantage in his home country.

Her father arrived in Brooklyn with a job offer that was rescinded when he reported for his first day at a manufacturing plant ("Don't need you anymore, pal"). Anxious for survival, he joined the hordes of immigrant taxi drivers, forever leaving behind his paneled office and legions of underlings in the former British colonial administration center of Ravalapur.

Her mother sometimes spoke of another version of her father, one who had managed an entire metallurgy operation with boiling temper and lashing impatience. But Meena only remembered a man who drove a night taxi, who smiled tenderly and placed her on his lap to complete *The New York Times* crossword left behind during his latest shift. "Solving this crossword means that we are Americans, Meena!" They faced each one with determination.

On her eleventh birthday, five years after arriving in their new country, Meena's father asked her to choose her annual treat, then departed in his taxi to fetch her favorite ice cream. She waved at him from the window of the walkup, then danced in anticipation of the rare treat she requested.

Meena remembered little else about that day. She could not even picture her father's face or body in the hospital bed, only herself sitting for an eternity in the ICU waiting room, watched over by kind nurses. And she remembered rocking, white-knuckled, grasping the handles of her chair, trying to breathe through the weight on her chest, the one that whispered, *Why, why did you send your father away?*

Afterwards, kind neighbors looked in on them occasionally, but Meena's mother, fortunately educated in an English medium school, pushed through the days on her own, finding work as a receptionist at a local bank until she could enter the teller's program. They moved from sublet to sublet until Meena's mother could gain a foothold. "Work hard, Meena," her mother admonished. "There is no security without working hard."

Meena did not need reminding. Life seemed harrowing, and Meena intended to ensure her future stability. She excelled at school, eschewing all social activities, befriending a small cadre of equally driven students, and easily won a full scholarship to a small engineering college near the city. *Work hard, Meena, work hard.* It was a mantra in her head, a verbal talisman to ward off disaster.

During the first week of class, Meena sat perched on the edge of her seat, anxious not to miss a single nuance of the lecture. A few weeks later, relieved that she was capable of handling the challenging material, she finally relaxed back in her chair and took a quick glance around the room at her fellow students.

A male student in the last row caught her eye and winked.

Meena's forehead creased. She looked behind her to find the intended recipient. It couldn't be Meena herself, dressed in jeans and an oversized turtleneck, hair coiled in a bun at the top of her head. Furtively, she looked up at him again.

Wink! Astonished by his brazenness, she frowned at him and turned again to the lecture. Afterwards, he crossed the large hall and held out his hand to her. "Vishal," he said brightly.

Eventually, he talked her into a celebratory coffee after the first set of exams. She slowly learned that his friendliness was accompanied by intelligence that grasped concepts and calculations instantly, hands that built and tested efficiently. He was "second generation," the son of doctors, comfortable, ebullient, happy. To her, he was a window into an alternative universe, one full of ease and laughter.

It surprised Meena how quickly he'd won her trust, then her love — through sheer insouciance, it seemed. She worried what her mother would say when she took her new fiance home just four months after starting college. But her mother looked relieved and embraced Vishal tightly.

Vishal had held Meena securely whenever she talked about her father, whenever she wept that she was responsible. "No, darling Meena, no, that's not how life works." Sometimes she asked him wonderingly, "Why? Why do you love me?" He would shake his head at her, his eyes crinkled and bemused, before responding seriously, "As soon as I saw you, I knew I had to take care of you. I knew I had to make you laugh." Meena breathed her relief, every time.

Tiferet

Slowly, she had placed all the pieces of herself and her pain into his open palms.

Meena now dropped her face into her hands. Courtship, engagement, marriage, job. What had been the purpose of it all? She followed her thoughts into darker hallways, and all those pieces of herself, once placed in Vishal's safekeeping, seemed once again scattered at her feet.

She watched the shadows in the room elongate.

"Meena!"

This time, she was ready. Meena moved close to the lamp, forced her body to calm, to breathe; she would not lose her chance again.

"Vishal! I shouldn't have made you take the car. You were relaxing, and I... I..." Meena choked. "The truck hit you, and it's all so senseless." Meena could not continue.

"Meena, are you listening?" Vishal's voice sounded desperate. "There's no more time. I learned something, and I need to tell you: the same things happen to us, over and over, until we forgive."

"Oh, Vishal, please forgive me."

"Meena, Meena, of course I forgive you. That's not what I mean. Forgive yourself — for what happened to your father. And to me. Meena..."

"Vishal!"

The lamp extinguished. Meena felt his words stir into all of her pain, neutralizing its acid, little by little.

She picked up the lamp and imagined her beloved holding onto some silken tether to her realm of existence, ensuring she received what she needed to endure the minutes and days ahead, reminding her of the deep, wide love she possessed in an uncertain world.

Meena wondered what it had cost Vishal, wondered at the torment of existing between spaces. She watched the oil tip into her palm and mix with her tears, felt the concoction fuse and meld, and she wished him well in his journey onward.

POETRY

Intrusion

Priscilla Orr

On the shoreline, you surface
if only in memory, love akin to infrared
waves—invisible to the human eye.
Where do I hold you within me?

Not in my heart, organ that will beat
a billion times in this life.
Encoded and stored like light waves
or x-rays that move through soft tissue,

sear into bone, you are always there.
Oblivious, my terrier burrows his nose in wet sand,
then moves into a full body dig. On the ride home,
he'll carry the remnants of dead crab and seaweed,

and snore in his car-seat from sweet exhaustion.
Will you recede into the neural network of my mind
while I drive into the imperceptible blue waves of dusk?

NONFICTION

It's a Great Life if You Don't Weaken

Susan Pohlman

It was late in the afternoon. I was leaving the Piazza di Michelangelo to hike down the hillside of Oltrarno toward the center of Florence when the church bells began to toll. They marked the top of the hour, primal and alluring. Looking for the source, I spied a sign that pointed left, upward, to the basilica of San Miniato al Monte. I had a dinner reservation and I needed to leave soon to make it—but an opportunity to explore was at hand. Right here, right now. Chances of coming back here this week were slim, and what if my propensity to be timely and disciplined (a.k.a. dull and boring) prevented me from experiencing something significant? Who knew what lay above?

If I had learned anything from my year of living dangerously in Genoa, it was to let go of "shoulds" and follow paths that called to me. Almost without fail, a lovely or amazing discovery would reveal itself. Something important.

I figured that my daughter, Katie, and my friend, Annie, could entertain each other until I arrived at the restaurant, so I headed up the hill another quarter of a mile. Soon, I arrived at a set of steep white stone stairs that ascended to the church, its Romanesque facade a combination of alabaster and moss-green marble framed against a deepening indigo sky. Above the center door, gold mosaics shimmered, as if radiating a light of their own.

A few tourists stood near the curb. They wondered aloud if they should exert themselves for "just another church." They were tired—hadn't they climbed enough stairs for one day? They were unaware of the gift of perspective. That the higher you rise above the fray, the sharper what really matters to you will come into focus. I didn't tell them. Why let their whining ruin my view?

I gritted my teeth and began to climb. *Take me higher*, I thought to myself between breaths. *Enchant me.* Soon I was standing on flat land, beholding an even more amazing vista of the Tuscan countryside. Gazing westward, I willed the scenery to imprint itself upon me as the sun melted down the sky. An elderly monk tottered by in an ivory robe cinched at the waist by a brown rope, his shadow trailing behind him. He seemed to float; an angel with a cane.

From this vantage point I saw that the church was only one portion of a compound that included an ancient monastery. I decided that I could peek inside the church after dark, but I wanted to walk the grounds as the sun set. To my left was a brick archway and a path that led around the side of the property. I headed through it, expecting to see gardens and perhaps a shrine or two. Instead, I found the entrance to the cemetery to end all cemeteries. Nothing like walking into a graveyard to dampen a fine mood.

I did not climb the hillside to work through my thoughts of death, but there I stood, literally, in the midst of it. Again, it seemed that my teacher had appeared, deftly luring me here to press my nose against my greatest fear. Because I have learned that the only way to deal with pain is to walk right through it, I accepted the invitation to explore my feelings.

I took a centering breath and moved forward. Took the step I had been avoiding. I began by wandering slowly, carefully treading around the maze of tombs. The cemetery was crowded with headstones; sculptures; carvings of cherubs, crosses and children; obelisks and columns balanced on pedestals; and full-scale angels, who guarded tombs while weeping and praying. Sculptures of grieving mothers pleaded, reached, and wailed. A life-sized muscled warrior lay, face down in surrender across one grave, clutching a victory torch, extinguished. There was a bust of a dashing gentleman in a top hat and a cloaked woman crying on the steps of a mausoleum, strewn with silk lilies and ceramic roses. Hanging lamps, brassy and rusted, were lit with tiny electric bulbs that grew bright as the sunlight faded.

This was not just any old graveyard; this was a prayer. A mesmerizing tribute to life, brilliant and brimming with sentiment. I have long understood that Italians are a passionate people. Their joie de vivre had lifted me from the darkest point of my life, but I did not know that they were also passionate about death. This was an outdoor museum of sepulchral artwork at its finest, the artistic rendering of the searing emotions that mark our lives.

A maroon jacket zigzagging slowly at the far end of the property caught my eye. From this distance, I could see that it belonged to a man, aged and crooked, carrying a brown paper bag. He bent for a moment, picked something off the ground, and placed it in his bag.

I drifted, studied, photographed, and in so doing began to get a sense of those buried there and those they left behind—variations of grays and whites in a dance of days gone by. Curiously, I didn't feel an absence of color. I felt all of them, every shade. I imagined blue and pink baby blankets and the sweet yellow crinoline of a preteen beauty. I glimpsed navy uniforms with gold buttons and black boots with worn heels and tattered laces. Around a corner, a sensible brown dress curtsied, boasting a collar of fine lace, and a trio of smoky, pin-striped suits pressed with

Tiferet

straight seams gathered to discuss the news of the day. I stared into framed photos fixed above chiseled names, loved ones with serious eyes and smiles edged in mystery. I was walking through a history book.

The wind rushed through the branches of the cypresses that stood guard across the rear of the property, speaking to me in the whispers of the dead. They were beautiful whispers, like the fragrance of orange blossoms. They said things like: *I have been loved; I was a hero to someone; I mattered; I have lived a life that deserves a headstone that cries for eternity.*

A few weeks ago, I pedaled my bike along a path near a cemetery in Arizona. I stopped for a moment to tie a shoelace that came undone and noticed a young woman on a bench with her head bent in prayer. I wondered who she was visiting, for whom she was aching. The cemetery, from my vantage point, was a green field with flat stones like shoe boxes lined in straight rows. It was neat, orderly, and sterile. It offended me, the way it erased lives. I want to mark the earth when I die. I don't want to politely disappear into a plot that bows to a lawn mower.

These last few years I have become increasingly beset with the subject of death. I have already begun to mourn the passing of my parents, my husband, my siblings and friends—and they are as alive as I am. Every day there is a moment when I tell myself that I now have one less opportunity to call my mother or my father, feel my husband's arms around me, hear my brothers' voices, exchange sweet sarcasm and laughter with a friend. Part of me wants to camp out in their guest rooms just to stare at them, to breathe in their essence.

Some days I call my parents, and while talking about things like grocery lists and brands of coffee, my heart screams "don't die!" so loudly that I cover the mouthpiece so they can't hear it. Another part of me wants to perish first so I don't have to bear the grief. I have borne all sorts of things in my life, but I honestly don't believe that I have the emotional strength for final good-byes. I just don't. I fear them with all of my being.

I read once that a person should be buried in a place where the earth knows them. That sentence made my mouth go dry, my stomach clench into a mass of granite. I didn't have a place that knew me. I was a rolling stone, even though I'd never wanted to roll in the first place. Sure, my childhood in New Jersey was long and steady, but my married life had taken me across the nation and overseas. My hometown cradled me for eighteen years, but that world had dissipated decades ago into a mist of remember-whens. My soul was homeless. I wondered if I should include a clause in my will that provided for a moving van to pick up my casket and move it every three years.

I stopped for a moment to catch my breath, looking to the horizon to steady myself. The shadows were lengthening, and, all of a sudden, eternity didn't look so far away. Still, I felt like an intruder. A show-off. Like I was parading my pumping heart, flaunting my warm skin. I stepped more carefully and respectfully through the graveyard, translating the inscriptions: *Rest In Peace; Sleeping With the Angels; Sadly Missed; In Loving Remembrance; In Memory Of; Eternally Loved.*

I think that headstones are only half-inscribed. One side should contain the name and dates that communicate a life span, but the other should be the real tribute. Aren't details the true measure of a life? *Beloved Father* says one thing, but, *Dad, I Can't Live Without Your Corny Jokes and the Sound of Your Footsteps Upon that Old Linoleum You Refused to Update,* says quite another. *Treasured Mother* is fine enough, but, *Mom, Whose Laughing Eyes Will I Search for in a Crowded Room When Someone Makes a Social Gaffe or Dresses Inappropriately?* captures so much more.

Two summers ago, my mother and I took a trip to Troy, New York to attend a family celebration. My mother spent her childhood in the nearby small suburb of Watervliet. As children, we used to love making the three-hour drive there from New Jersey so she could take us on the grand tour of her youth. We'd drive by the brick house on Second Avenue where her grandmother had lived, and the second-story flat where she'd spent her early years. We'd pass the Catholic high school where she was once crowned prom queen, and the nursing school she attended down the street from Rensselaer Polytechnic Institute, where she met my dad. She'd show us the train tracks where the tramps huddled around fires near the Erie Canal and retell the story of the notorious George Van Auken, the hobo she always said we'd end up like if we didn't work hard in school. Then we'd pay tribute to the house where Frances, her best friend and partner in crime, had lived. We'd end the tour by ordering footlongs at the hot-dog stand known for the best chili dogs on the planet.

During those trips, my mother always made a point of driving us to the pastoral cemetery where my grandparents, Hester and Millard, were buried. We'd file out of the white station wagon and make an afternoon of it, imagining the life stories associated with the headstones we passed as we clambered up the hill searching for the two inscriptions that would call us to silence and remembrance.

That morning two years ago, after coffee, my mother and I set off on our usual pilgrimage. We drove down Route 787 toward Albany Rural Cemetery, chatting about life, but as we exited the highway my mother unexpectedly pulled to the side of the ramp and said, "Let's not go."

"What?" I said, blinking in disbelief. "Of course we have to go. It might be years before we get back to the East Coast."

"Grandma wouldn't mind," she said, her hands gripping the steering wheel.

Tiferet

"I know, but... it's tradition." What was going on?

"She's not actually there, you know."

"Mom, we can't be this close and turn around." I needed to go. I loved my grandparents, and if I lived closer, I would have made this journey often. It was one of those cemeteries that would be a hit in Hollywood. Mighty oaks and maples, hills, wandering paths, and old stone markers with names half-worn. They weren't tombstones to me; they were touchstones. I needed to touch them.

Looking back, I wondered if my insistence had been wrong, if I was pushing something that was too painful. Maybe it wasn't about the sadness of her parents being gone, but the fear of her own mortality. There are some things that you just don't discuss with your parents when you are driving toward a cemetery. We turned right on Cemetery Avenue and drove through the iron gates. The property was considerable, and I could never remember where to turn, but my mother always knew the exact spot to park the car. I don't think you ever forget the place where your parents are buried.

We climbed a slope through unkempt grass and scanned the headstones. Irish names, all of them: Doyle, MacDermott, O'Callahan, Sweeney, O'Leary. I heard the soft sigh of heartache, a heavy stillness, a sacred hush.

"It's over there." My mother pointed as she walked ahead. I stopped as I passed other grave sites and righted a few flower pots that had fallen sideways. As I anchored the pots as best I could, I saw Mom pause in a way that made it clear she had found them. Her hesitant posture held a weight that only those who grieve can fully comprehend. I wanted to give her some privacy, so I busied myself arranging a Mrs. Maguire's faded yellow silk snapdragons that had been scattered by the wind.

From my kneeling position, I spied a splotch of bright red a few feet away. I reached for it and found a silk poppy, its black button center tangled in the grass. I looked around for its source but could see no other toppled vases. Then I stood and saw another poppy a few yards ahead, and then two more flat against the base of my grandmother's headstone. I gathered them, incredulously, like Hansel and Gretel finding the trail of pebbles that led them home.

I held out my cupped hands to show my mother. "Look," I said, both of our eyes glistening with tears. The red poppies said everything we could not. "I guess she is here after all."

I chose the red poppy as my symbol after I published my first book, *Halfway to Each Other*. In one of the chapters, I speak about my grandmother and the hat she used to wear every Easter. We thought it was exquisite and daring, covered in red silk poppies that bloomed above her silver curls. A hat that had turned her into a fashion statement with an exclamation point.

I searched the hillside and peered into the branches of the towering trees, expecting to see her blue eyes and sweet smile. And I was sure that I caught a drift of the pungent scent of tobacco. Good old Gramps; I could still smell his pipe twenty-five years after it went out.

My mother knelt, gently brushed away some dead leaves, and cleaned the tiny plot of land that held her parents and grandparents. We stood there for the longest time without a word. Because, really, what could words capture?

Our walk back to the car was silent but full. Part of me didn't want to leave. I've always suspected that there is some unexplained space between us and those who have passed. I wrestle with this feeling. These are the moments when I feel like I have brushed against this dimension, pierced its membrane. I find comfort in the unexplainable sense of presence, the ease of it, the lack of fear.

As my mother jangled her keys and unlocked the car door, our eyes met over the roof. We smiled and nodded as she recited an old family saying, the one we always share at the end of conversations with no resolution or moments beyond words. It's the same saying she and her mom shared for decades, when life got crazy or they simply needed to let off some steam.

"Well… it's a great life if you don't weaken," she said. We laughed the way we always do, and I loved her then more than ever. I think that was the moment I began to mourn, the moment I realized that one day it would be me unlocking the car door and saying this to my own children.

I broke from my reverie when the bells of San Miniato began to toll again. I watched them swing back and forth in the old tower above me, the clappers clanging this way and that. An hour had passed effortlessly; the light was almost gone. I made my way around the side of the church with a new understanding of why Italians cater to their dead: because in so doing, they offer the living comfort and hope. This cemetery was eerily alive, and for the first time I understood how there can be death in life and life in death.

Suddenly, the man in maroon was behind me. Unnerved, I turned to see if it was a coincidence or if he was following me. Our eyes met, and then his traveled to the camera, heavy around my neck.

"Perché le fotografie?" he demanded in a gravelly voice that was less than friendly. *Why the photographs?*

"Rispetto!" *With respect!* I quickly showed him my last shot of an exquisite sculpture of a mother and child.

He peered at the image and then back at me. There was something off about his energy, but he didn't seem dangerous. His clothes were clean, though tattered, and his paper bag was filled with litter.

Tiferet

"Okay?" I asked.

He nodded and pointed to a stand of trees along the rim. "Mia moglie c'è." *My wife is there.*

"Mi dispiace." *I'm sorry.*

"Il suo tempo," he said matter-of-factly. *Her time.* He held out the paper bag and smiled. "Lavori domestici. La mia casa ora." *Housework. This is my home now.*

My heart lurched. Again, a change in perspective had granted me some peace. As Teilhard de Chardin said, "We are not human beings on a spiritual journey. We are spiritual beings on a human journey." When we become aware of our spirituality and the way we connect with life's mysteries, our sorrows sprout wings and seek flight.

I walked to the front edge of the church grounds to catch the edge of twilight over the layered hills. A hazy darkness rose from the countryside, exploding into pinks and golds. It was so beautiful that I pinched myself.

As the horizon burned down to a ginger strip, points of light began to dot the landscape as far as I could see. Spotlights illuminated the Duomo, the Palazzo Vecchio, and other landmarks in Florence I had yet to explore. Streetlights shone along the Arno river, shops and restaurants glimmered bright welcomes, and the windows of homes busy with dinner preparations radiated. It was the glow of the living.

Night must fall for us to see and appreciate light. In one of those glowing pinpoints, my best friend and my daughter were waiting for me, and I had a feeling that I would have more than one glass of deep-red wine. I would silently toast all of those who had gone before, but mostly, I would toast to life and the joy that was all around and within me.

There are many things about death I don't need to know the answer to right now. I have to trust that the gift of understanding will grace me when I need it. I don't know if I will lie across a loved one's tomb or weep for eternity or stand tall in thanksgiving for having known such fine people. I'll probably do a completely messed-up and unattractive combination of all three, but I know I will get through it with God's love.

I carefully made my way down the white stone steps of San Miniato and turned right down the winding street to the wide stairs that would take me back to the Arno and across the Ponte alle Grazie. Falling into line behind three twenty-something girls, arms linked and laughing the deep, free laughter of youth, I buttoned my jacket, tightened my scarf, and smiled at the stars that twinkled above, thankful for my great life while reminding myself, for the umpteenth time, not to weaken.

POETRY

Spring Rain

Elaine Koplow

I take the dirt path
alongside trees whose
ivied limbs canopy the road
shielding me from the last
of a light spring shower.
Here the clearing opens
and spreads itself wide
onto a rocky bank
where I will take my lunch.
From my stony perch
I watch
the way reed stubble
beards the pond
how clouds above yield
unregretfully to blue.
Warmrh rises and lingers
in the still, expectant
air. A light breeze circles once
like an afterthought, passes
through. Around me
the self-renewal of water
insects, moss, of buds,
even the earth itself. All
seem to welcome it,
to bask in it.
I watch and wonder
if it pains them too.

POETRY

The World Soul

Ray Cicetti

Alone in the restaurant, I turn to an article about how we all share a world soul that runs through everything, doesn't come or go but shows up moment after moment as compassion or awe. It says it is like that ocean-like swell in the chest at the sight of a sunrise, death, or a newborn child.

I look up from my magazine, curious about this possibility, to see an inebriated man refused another drink by the bartender. I watch two Hispanic waitstaff, invisible to most, laugh with patrons as they clean up dirty plates and glasses from empty tables.

At the far end of the room, my waiter, in his starched white shirt and bow tie, now offers a young couple, unhappy with their meals, new ones for free. My heart lights up like a struck match when he lifts his head, turns toward me and smiles, as if responding to something we both feel, some invisible thread between us, so obvious it doesn't have a name and no one even thinks about it.

NONFICTION

That Old Time Religion

Reg Darling

The various words and names used to describe deities (God, Allah, Jehovah, Jayzus!, Atman, The Great Pumpkin, etc.) have so many different meanings that they are functionally meaningless. That's why so many people, especially those who already harbor too many strange voids within, feel compelled to personalize them— to give deities not only names, but often also faces, personalities, and even genders.

[I confess I don't understand the heartfelt urgency of their need. I've never felt it. My heart has been broken many times by both certainties and doubts, but never by mystery.]

Though comforting illusions can seem sweetly benign, when great mysteries are synthetically concretized, they encourage narrow-mindedness and diminish compassion.

[Human violence didn't come from Pleistocene carnivorousness; it came from the angry gods of desert religions. It came from the civilized savagery of punished children.]

I find most vocal prayers (forgivably) embarrassing. It seldom occurs to the perpetrators that their prideful proclamations of humility and gratitude offered up as barter for divine favors might be socially awkward for people too honest to bow their heads for the charade.

[Generally speaking, supplication is unhealthy, though it is certainly understandable if you're down and bleeding. It's not good to have a beggared relationship with a person, god, or nature. The human spirit is not improved by groveling, and wounded pride is a poor substitute for humility.]

I am one of those who furtively gaze unbowed about the room, hoping the display of piety will be brief. Even when merciful brevity is not granted, the offense is readily forgiven ("they know not what they do"). But still, life and love fully provide plenty of sad sighs without help from the rude presumptuousness of Christian displays of voodoo-lite.

My refusal to bow my head and pretend is neither prideful nor defiant (well, maybe it's a little defiant); I just can't fucking do it.

[Inhibition and honesty become allies in the absence of desire.]

If I were a more patient man, the inability of believers to understand the difference between disbelief and non-belief would be less vexing.

[Although ritual and ceremony savored deeply, but held lightly, can be therapeutic and often more, a person who thinks they can change reality with magical incantations is delusional. There are better things to aspire to than becoming some sort of minor league Merlin. Demeaning the intrinsic wonder of conscious attention with

Tiferet

fantasies of magic will lead away from possibilities of transcendence, not toward them.]

The real value of religion is simply as a means to nurture an affectionate reciprocal relationship with reality. An affectionate reciprocal relationship with reality is a sound foundation for unconditional kindness.

[Religion isn't the only way to have such a relationship with reality, but it works well for many people across a broad spectrum of intelligence, talent, and education. The downside is that it is easily weaponized by demagogues.]

When religion oversteps the bounds of this fundamental purpose, the result is rather like intestinal contents leaking into the abdominal cavity—there is a deadly, raging infection. Seriously ugly shitloads of anger fester into self-destructive fevers of violence and stupidity. This often results in cruel fools invested with great power and atrocities committed (or at least financed) by people whose hearts are fundamentally kind.

[Dogma doesn't merely encourage violence; it is violence.]

There are times of inner clarity manifest in outward perceptions (mostly in encounters with art, nature, and loving sex) when I seem to witness the divine at work in the world.

[The above is a descriptive statement, not a prescriptive one.]

Both divinity and soul are necessary components of my expressive vocabulary. To arbitrarily constrain either with particularities of belief seems arrogant, presumptuous, and irreverent.

[Namaste.]

Peggy James   THE RETURNING LIGHT

POETRY

Long Overdue Letter to My Father

Tom Plante

I see your face in my mind's screening room,
the look of *what's going on in this kid's head?* that you gave me
during arguments before I hopped a Greyhound for California.
I left behind only assurances that I'd be back.

And I see your young smile in a souvenir photograph
from the House of O'Sullivan on Sunset Blvd.
when you were an Army trainee far from Brooklyn
before you were stationed in Panama to protect the canal.

The same eyes and smile that I last saw
when I flew in from Berkeley to be at your bedside.
One never knows, do one? as you used to say
were among your last words.

Snow fell that April night, a rare weekend blizzard.
The thick white quilt at the cemetery
meant extra duty for the gravediggers.
You would have been 101 yesterday.

I still see your face and knowing smile. I imagine
you watched me when I returned to the job
in California, only to be asked by a worker,
How was your vacation?

NONFICTION

The Existential Dog

Daniel Menaker

Maxwell has eaves of fur that half-cover his eyes. Unless we barber them a little, they grow more eaves-esque as his last professional grooming recedes into the past. But all the Tibetan-terrier sources say he can see perfectly well through the curtain, anyway. What gets me more than that—what gets me to the point of existential bafflement–is that forelocked or not, dogs don't see colors the way we do. They see fewer colors. Just as we don't see ultraviolet, dogs can't distinguish red, green, or yellow objects according to their color.

Who can see ultraviolet colors, you might ask. In that unlikely event, I would answer: Birds. Birds can also see far more colors than we do. Or far more distinct shades of colors than we can. And cats can hear 1.6 octaves above what we can hear—up to 64 kHz, which is an octave above what even dogs can hear, which in turn is above what we can hear. Fish can see polarized light. We can't. Caterpillars can "see" only darkness and brightness.

Back to Maxwell: he and his species famously have a sense of smell at least ten thousand times more acute than ours. This explains why when I am in the kitchen eating peanut butter out of the jar and he is practically in the Philippines, he will nose the three molecules of Skippy in the air that reach the exquisitely sensitive receptors in his snout and shamble into the kitchen, feigning deference, sit the apparently requisite three feet away, and gaze at me in that maddeningly patient way of his, until I give in.

In the breath of patients, dogs can detect the odor of the metabolic byproducts of breast cancer. A fellow-oncodogist detected the scent of melanoma in the skin of a patient pronounced cancer-free by doctors. A police dog can sniff out a small amount of marijuana in a plastic bag immersed in gasoline *inside a gas tank*. Alexandra Horowitz's recent book, *Inside of a Dog*, as well as other books and articles, have documented these olfactory amazements almost to a surfeit, but they continue to amaze.

I rehearse these sensory phenomena to sort of get my philosophical motor running. I shift into first: is Maxwell seeing reality less "accurately" than I am? Is he smelling it more accurately? Is the caterpillar seeing reality less "really" than I am? Is what a cat hears better—that is, more full and correct—than what I hear? Now, into second: can any creature's experience of Reality be said to be in any way "better"—more accurate—than any other's? Finally, into high: how, given the subjectivity—the species-centric nature—of the perceptions of different creatures that are capable of perceiving anything—can there be said to be anything fully and truly objective about anything?

Tiferet

You would think that anyone who has left Phil 101 behind by a matter
of sixty years would forever stay away from all those slippery slopes and dead ends
and circularities. But for some, if not many, if not most of us, it seems that these
mysteries, these ultimately probably unanswerable questions, resurface as The End
gets a little closer. Well, O.K.—for me, a lot closer. Why?

In my own case, contemplating the mysteries has indirectly lessened my
fear of The End. If Reality, whatever it is, is un-pin-downable—variable according
species, with the human, technologically-boosted version of it being perhaps the
most extensive but still almost certainly nothing like bedrock—that variability
somehow eases, at least for me, the prospect of permanent departure. I'm guessing
this easing verges on a kind of homegrown Buddhism. Something to do with
illusoriness, impermanence, detachment.

For Maxwell, no such fantods. Everything is real, permanent, and attached.
Nothing like our consciousness and reason interposes itself between him and the
hydrant, between him and the muskrat whose neck he recently and so primally
snapped, between him and the aroma of peanut butter, coming to him in parts per
trillion.

To continue with these reflections:

No matter how somnolent Maxwell may be, this olfactory genius of his
switches him instantly into to alert mode whenever I go near 1) the refrigerator; 2)
the cupboard where we keep the snacks for human beings; 3) the cupboard where
we keep his own delectables, and, of course; 4) anyplace that may store peanut
butter. He even craves the "dental chews."

You know the drill, if you have a dog, or if you have ever seen a dog in this
situation. Here is our drill, anyway: Maxwell switches to On from his default Sleep
Setting and walks over to me where I stand in the kitchen. He always takes up a
mendicant's respectful distance, about three feet, and just sits there gazing at me
quietly. This quiet is deafening. He just looks at me. The way Zeus looked at Leda.
Well, let me try again. The way I look at bacon, when someone else controls it. The
way an orphan ragamuffin looks in at the window of a bakery. The way I look at
the first-class cabin from the economy section, even the comfort economy section.
(Comfort economy; an oxymoron.)

It used to be thought that dogs, or the original dog, domesticated itself, by
doing a little work, and conning human beings into feeding it and giving it shelter.
That it was the original con artist of affection. In this connection, I remember once,
at the publishing house where I worked, somebody brought up a book proposal
about dogs as The First Scammers. Our publisher rejected the idea, on the grounds
that it seemed awfully speculative—or so she said, at first. The person who presented
the proposal kept bringing it up and kept being interrupted, with increasing
irritation, by our boss. Finally she said, "OK, Scott, I have a dog, and I refuse to
accept this idea. I know my dog loves me. I know he is not exploiting me. So we are
not going to acquire this book."

I thought at the time that dogs as con artists was a reasonable theory. It fit into my intermittent worldview of every creature looking for Darwinian advantage, its prey, or a soft touch—like, say, a serotonin-starved human being whose neurotransmitter system might be vulnerable to a lick on the hand, a paw shake, a boisterous, joyful greeting at just the turn of a door knob, or what seemed to be a loving gaze. But then, not too long ago, scientists somehow measured the chemical activity not only in the brain of a human responding to a dog but of a dog responding to a human. And it turns out that a dog also gets a blast of serotonin when he looks at his master. So it's a two-way street of affection. My boss was right, as she often was.

But I'm sorry—you can't convince me that Maxwell's apparently loving regard of me when I am near something he wants to ingest but can't get at himself isn't manipulative. I still think the conning theory holds at least a teaspoon of water. I have a friend whose dog runs into the kitchen whenever he's in there and says "Oops!"

So, do I give him forty-five degrees of a nice round McVittie's digestive? I do. Do I give him a cheddar shard? I do. Does he get to lick the ice-cream spoon? He does. Does he get a few Milk Bone parti-colored treats if he lies down and crosses one paw over the other? He does. Do we understand each other? Probably not, but that's the point, maybe—maybe that's why we keep dogs. We look at them and know that they look at us with very limited understanding, however rewarding it may be. And that's how we look at the universe, if we have the wonder and humility to do so.

Anyway, yes, dogs may really love us, but they are still opportunists. And we may love them, but we are still, to however limited an extent, suckers.

Lucky dog.

More about the give-and-take between a particular dog and his human:

Maxwell does the following tricks on command: sits, lies down, crosses one paw over the other (this is my own genius idea, though I'm sure millions of other masters—that is, servants—have had same idea), goes around me in a circle to the right, goes around me in a circle to the left, shakes hands with his right paw, jumps the gun and offers his left paw unbidden unless I caution him not to, which he obeys in an obviously exasperated or forbearing way, rolls over, puts his front paws up on an arm held parallel to the floor and gets a treat over the arm and then gets one under it when you say "over" and "under" in that order (and will even do it in reverse order), goes through between your legs and comes back through them and turns in place 360 degrees, stands on his hind legs and pirouettes 360 degrees.

He could learn more tricks, I'm sure, but at this middle-age point I figure that as I am who I am if not past it at seventy-five, Maxwell is who he is at seven times seven equals forty-nine, deserves the respect of his maturity, and should not be sent back to circus school. I do wish he would come whenever he is told to instead of just as a velleity. We have bought gourmet "training treats" as an inducement to obey the command, "Maxwell, come!" every time. But if there is some vile, dead animal in the woods that he feels required to roll and get stinky in, or a UPS guy whom he sees as an intruder to be deafened with barking, forget it, Zuke's Roasted Pork Recipe Mini Naturals and Tricky Trainer Chewy Liver Flavor Wheat- and Corn-Free Training Treats notwithstanding.

Zuke is evidently a paradigm of obedience in Durango, Colorado, who, according to the packaging, "sits, stays, and focuses—ready to learn or just enjoy a healthy treat for being such a good boy"" Well, you go, Zuke. Maxwell will be too busy dirt-swimming with his two front paws after a mole who just scooted under the stone bench in our yard.

Despite these complaints and even though I am foregoing most further trick teaching, I am hoping that Maxwell will do one more thing I find myself silently asking him to do. And that is to let me Lie Down for good before he does.
Stay, Max!

POETRY

A Million Names

Wryly T. McCutchen

There are a million ways to name pain and grief.

A name is
an anchor, is a hitching
post in the pitching
vertigo of ocean.

On my world
all of the forests are burning
down. There are holes
in the sky. The waters,
they are rising.

If it's a question of time
travel, tectonic drift will
shift geography against you.
Even if your switch
is jammed into a single setting
forward and steady.
Name the birds.
Name the landscape.

Even islands die after some time.
Name them anyway.
Our throats carry a water
table of contents.
It's how we find our way
how we fill the time, how we soak
the wounds, the way we cure
and salt the meat for winter.

There are a million ways to name pain and grief.

An atlas for all that is
temporal. To name
something is to hang

Tiferet

a stopwatch around its neck.
I do not think I understand death
but death understands me
understands us
landscape and all.

In a universe of rootless
loam, it's dreadfully
simple to get off
at the wrong stop. To
leave early with someone
you love. Or because it's too dark,
too rainy to see the street signs.

You have to remember the names
or reinvent them and hope that
the landscape matches the incantations
you cast into its dark spaces.
We are all bending along, until
we burn the forests down, until
the oceans come for us and
the islands are pulled under.

There are a million ways to name pain and grief.

When the land can no longer speak,
they will wait
in the sea
like a tribe of glistening mermaids.

POETRY

Contents

Wryly Tender McCutchen

I contain multiplication tables
I contain water tables
I contain water chestnuts
I contain a waterfall of chest
I contain forty-two moons
I contain seven times six is
I contain the oceans constricting
I contain tidefuls of fish
I contain the algorithm
   the melody
I contain the smooth stone talk
I contain flirtatious waves and vicious undertow
I contain skates and rays
I contain many more teeth than bones
I contain magic and matter which is 99% nothing at all
I contain the white space the big bang left over
I contain mass uncontrasted
I contain fluids
   mucous membranes
   all that is
   disgusting
   divine
   tantalizing
I contain many breaches
I contain the belly of a whale
I contain distress intestinal
I contain woods and winds
I contain sharps and flats
I contain hashtags and stilettos
I contain portraits and landscapes
I contain maps
   globes
   atlases
   continents drawn disproportionately
I contain where there be monsters
I contain the jungle of trauma

Tiferet

I contain the fresh darkness I remember and the ruptures that I forgot
I contain the formula for recovery
I contain the capacity to heal
I contain patience
I contain principles of uncertainty
I contain postulates
   theorems thick enough to swim through
I contain ash
   the seeming motionlessness of the earth
I contain sprained ankles
   crutches in the pouring rain
I contain the heavy burden of whimsy
I contain joint pain
I contain joint smoke
I contain a bowlful of cherries
I contain stained fingertips and dark pits
I contain spit
I contain humor
I contain vitriol
I contain sight
I contain undocumented senses
I contain pots boiling over
I contain the heat and homogenizing force of written history
I contain the waiting and unwritten
I contain already
   the wisdom in the lessons
   I'm learning and unlearning
I contain negotiation
I contain all that has passed and is passing
I contain new years
I contain old ears
I contain the sins that I borrowed
I contain all of the blue in the universe

Tiferet Tifs

We are delighted to share our latest installment of Tiferet "Tifs". While a "tiff" is defined as a "petty argument", a "Tif" is anything but petty—it is a short exploration of a deeply meaningful subject. In this issue, writers have explored the timely, powerful, word "Transformation". For more Tifs, please visit www.tiferetjournal.com.

The Grandmother of Clay Might Grow Angry
An excerpt from *The Ocarina Road*, a memoir in progress

Anita Feng

I am a jealous guardian. A light sleeper. As I have said many times before, pottery cannot be made without my permission. Some might saunter by and just see an outcrop of flinty rock poking through the tall grasses. But that would be me, and I am jealous of what I have made and what I love.

What you see (or don't see) are my shoulders hunched around this hoard of clay at my feet, here at the water's edge. And my eyes are everywhere. Those white veins running through the rock—those are my teeth.

For billions of years I've been grinding my teeth in my sleep, shattering mountains in my jaws. And that's because I'm jealous of the wind, envious of the rain, and tired of the rivers that come to steal my clay away. So when some bright-eyed and ignorant child comes along with the intention to just take some, you can believe that I will let her know the price. And it comes with warnings.

Clay comes out of my womb. Whether it lives or dies is in your hands. Be humble. Be careful. Be reckless. Be brave.

Tiferet Tifs

Winter's Tears
Georgiana Nelsen

The constant drip of melting icicles perforates the snow exactly three feet from the outside walls of the Cape Cod. Laney presses her nose against the window where she watches, exactly three feet up from where her feet touch the floor.

"Time to fix that."

"Don't break them, Mommy" she says, tugging on my sleeve.

I don't like knocking them down either. I like the way the sun refracts through the fringe of prisms, a rainbow dance on the walls inside. I wish I could tear along the dotted line they create and place the moment in her baby book.

Instead, I explain leaky roofs, and how icicles can hurt someone if they fall. I tell her there will be new ones tomorrow, and give her crayons and paper. "Draw them for me?" I wonder how she will color the ice.

The rake leans against the brick, and its tines ring like an ill-tuned guitar when strummed against the crystalline spikes. I step back quickly to keep from being stabbed as the icicles release. They plunk into the snow, but not before sending cold drips down the splintered handle of the rake and up my sleeve.

Tiferet Tifs

Becoming as Destruction
Katharine Coldiron

It was Leslie Scalapino, in *Dahlia's Iris*, who pointed out to me that in transition from caterpillar to butterfly, the entity must destroy itself in order to transform. The butterfly that becomes is not the caterpillar that went into the cocoon; they are two different creatures. Two bodies. One is "before," and the other "after," but the only relationship they bear to each other is the covering that one creature built and the other broke out of.

It's an attractive metaphor, this transition from a common crawling thing to a creature of flight and beauty, but it involves self-inflicted violence far beyond what humans—who grow from a small self to a large self, retaining spine and nerves and hair follicles—can comprehend. The mother-body makes something new within, and physicians will be able to see that journey even if the mother cannot speak for herself. But the mother-body does not destroy itself in order to become, and a caterpillar-body does.

What a wonder that this fact does not fill us with existential terror. Instead, we use butterflies as metaphors for the beautiful self, emerging from imaginal goo. Never considering what must be destroyed in order to become.

All the Moments Before
Thelma Wurzelbacher

Mildred, my neighbor, friend, and ex-con, lies elevated and commanding for her last seven hours. The hospice team and I will honor every wish.

Her face is vintage 1920, a landscape of memories, cheeks tinted by fever. Thick silver hair, military cut, is ear length. Beneath the slimy colorless oxygen tether, Chapstick smothered lips struggle to whisper. Her Catherine-the-Great nose relaxes as chemical mixed air streams inward; the bulbous wart no longer matters.

Beneath a wild garden of pale brow hairs, her green eyes with a vertical brown streak in one still hold their sneaky strength. She's like a night-seeing cat. Few noticed her well honed skill of lying about mistakes, significant or nonessential, glancing sideways to fabricate. No one has ever seen tears, although the possibilities are many: finding her beloved boss dead, stabbing of her childhood playmate, pushing the office mail cart after retirement age, robbed while in her home.

Crossed and quieted hands, centered over her chest, rest on the white shroud-looking blanket. Given her lifelong habit, all ten nails are perfectly manicured, intact, kept spear-like for gouging thieves and suspected assailants.

She only needs quality polish so she can stop the clock.

Tiferet Tifs

The Women Who Love Me
LaCoya Katoe

The women who love me speak of their lives in past tense. They show me unfulfilled dreams balled between fingers they refuse to unfurl. What glimpses I get of them ooze out between their knuckles, snippets of who they might have been had they broken free. Before I put the pieces of their lives together, they snatch back these possibilities and hold them against their chests. "Too late for me," they say, "but you still have time." They lay pressure upon my heart like boulders; I must carry their burdens and my own. But the work of transformation is mine alone to do. They don't tell me that in order to transform, I'll nudge our boulders a centimeter at first, then an inch, and every time I think I've done work enough to slip from under them, they fall on me again. But I do my work—repetitively— in different cities, on different jobs, in the arms of different lovers. I celebrate the smallest victories and try not to tally my losses. When the boulders grow heavy again, I make new attempts at freedom, always praying palms up, fighting the urge to clasp my fingers around anyone I might become.

A Review of *Night Ladder*

BY ADELE KENNY

NIGHT LADDER
By Lois P. Jones
Glass Lyre Press
104 Pages
$16.00 Paperback
ISBN: 978-1941783375
To order: https://www.amazon.com/Night-Ladder-
Lois-P-Jones/dp/1941783376/ref=sr_1_1?ie=UTF8&
qid=1519147192&sr=8-1&keywords=night+ladder

Beginning with the stunning cover painting "Bearer of Wonderment," Lois P. Jones's newest collection is filled with "wonderment" borne by her poems. In these poems, meaning is positioned within compelling and complex imagery. Jones, even in the darkest sense, consistently honors life. She speaks to the dead (including Rilke, Lorca, and Picasso) and to the present and future through lines and impressions that blend organically, often incorporating imagery drawn from the natural world. For example, this section of "Rilke's Maid, Leni at the Little Castle of Schloss Berg":

> … this evening's
> new moon rises over the pine, your face riven
>
> by its light as you enter your world
> of shadows. I will be the spirit of your
>
> departed, aloft as a white moth in winter,
> more cumulus than bone.

There is wonderful sonic impression in these poems, an intense musicality often tapped out in iambs. There is also the enjoyment of various metrical arrangements mixed with effective use of alliteration and assonance, all of which result in a unique lyricism as in this excerpt from "Ouija":

You asked for an R, the ripening of olives
in your garden, a red-tailed hawk

angling over the road, the path
that took you down and away

from the empty room of the body.

Presented in four cohesive sections, the poems "speak" through places in which
the temporal and spiritual worlds meet. In this section from "Birthday," Jones
juxtaposes the "escape" of dreams (and innocence) to her own feelings on a
birthday when she was a child.

… How could I know that dreams escape
as alchemy? That time is not trapped beneath
a crystal dome but a night of humid air, the black snake's
smoke and hiss as it curls out of the tablet,
flames into a pharaoh's serpent as we watch charmed

in the alley. My sister kneels on cement snapping the paper
roll caps with a sharp rock, our noses stung with sulfur.
We are rockets fired from a glass Coke bottle, the pyrotechnic
possibility of flight. It is an hour, a joy of country
being born. A belief that beginnings made everything possible,
like life in a mother's womb.

And I thought it was all for me, born on a day when the night
splinters aflame in wonder,
unconcerned with what occupies the dark.

There are clarity, experimentation, and abundant being in these poems that
address the universal heart through the narrator's particular heart. Both the
down-to-earth and the mystical content of these poems take Jones's readers on
a journey into the inner and outer worlds of human experience. Percy Bysshe
Shelley, in "A Defense of Poetry," marks the poet as a prophet, a person who
"participates in the eternal, the infinite, and the one." Essentially, the poet, then,
is one who adds to our understanding of the human condition. Jones, in a very
modern and image-driven way, adds to our understanding of what it means to be

human. She leads her readers to a reminder of poetry's higher purpose: through poetry we can come to a better perception of our who we are. Consider this excerpt from "How She Paints Herself":

> Sometimes the yearning
> burns so fiercely
> it illumines a body
>
> worthy of Gnostic devotion.
> Better to paint one's self
> from the inside out
>
> better to believe in the light
> that limns the brush.
> Faith is in your hand—
>
> in the way you reveal yourself ...

Throughout this stunning collection, there are flashes of beauty, sorrow, yearning, and wisdom, all of which coexist in seamless harmony. These poems astonish and delight with their depth of understanding, their vitality and strength, and their technical adeptness. There is also within this collection a prevailing sense of human goodness and hope against all odds. As I read the last lines of the last poem, I couldn't help feeling that the collection comes to closure by symbolizing what this extraordinary book is all about, and that we, along with the Jones are dogwood blossoms "caught in the act of flying" and "adrift in the impermanence of dying."

> 3. Flower
>
> Look at these dogwood blossoms
> caught in the act of flying,
>
> white wings bent and touching
> in a flock of origami.
>
> They could be cranes adrift
> in the impermanence of dying.

Jones's poems remind us that the ways we imagine the past are closely linked to the ways we imagine the future and move into it. Free of familiar and mundane ways of seeing and imagining, Jones's elegant and evocative poems charge our imaginations and move us toward deeper and richer connections to ourselves, to one another, and to higher spiritual realities.

Five Mini Reviews

BY ADELE KENNY

WORLD ENOUGH AND TIME
By Mary Makofske
Kelsay Books
116 Pages
$17.00 Paperback
ISBN: 978-1945752605
To order: https://www.amazon.com/World-Enough-Time-Mary-Makofske/dp/1945752602/ref=sr_1_6?s=books&ie=UTF8&qid=1519151581&sr=1-6&keywords=world+enough+and+time

The poems in this collection are stunningly alive with intelligence, passion for life, and rich sonic impression. Skillfully crafted, each poem is accessible and engaging. As a collection, these poems offer readers an integrated whole of language, form, and meaning. The poems move with momentum in a distinct arc as this gifted poet illuminates and situates the harmonies inherent in being human. Throughout the collection, the imagery is fresh and often based in the natural world, as in these lines from "Call Me to Follow:"

> Call me from birdsong and sun on my back
> scent of cilantro and mint …
>
> Call me from the path through woods to a view of the lake
> from falcon's dive, from garter snake
> that lives among rocks by the waterfall

Mary Makofske calls to her readers. She is a poet who practices her craft with deftness and clarity. She translates experience into written language that speaks to objective reality and spiritual understanding—to a life truly lived and deeply perceived. This is a superb book!

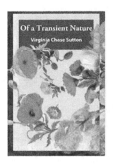

OF A TRANSIENT NATURE
By Virginia Chase Sutton
Knut House Press
143 Pages
$9.00 Paperback
ISBN: 978-0692645772
To order: https://www.amazon.com/TRANSIENT-NA-
TURE-Virginia-Chase-Sutton-ebook/dp/B01CRJSPHG/
ref=sr_1_1?ie=UTF8&qid=1519932632&sr=8-
1&keywords=transient+nature

This collection by Virginia Chase Sutton is supremely courageous. The interior "cloud" art by Philip Neil Mandel provides haunting reminders of the book's subject matter: a narrative of life's transitory nature. There is an unforgettable quality in every poem. There is also sensuality in the poems' attention to longing and desire. Most importantly, these poems are about the human spirit's persistence and resilience. Sutton's style is compact, direct, and carefully structured. Her imagery is specific and striking, richly textured with color, sensory detail, and strong emotional centers. Sutton writes with narrative proficiency and lyrical precision.

Prominent in the poems is a synthesis of the tragedy and the joy that are part of human reality. Elegiac as well as celebratory, these poems show us ways in which loss and change are navigated—the ways in which our spiritual and physical worlds are reconciled. Gritty, gutsy, and markedly vulnerable, these are the poems of a woman who comes face to face with herself and who dares to tell the story. This is a must-read collection of poems about living that will touch you with their strength.

From the poem, "Encountering Electro Convulsive Therapy:"

... Maybe ECT is not such a good idea
after all. Nothing else will work. We have tried everything,
the doc explains as he shuffles my release papers.
I am thinking about poems and paintings,

you know, art. Only a few patients realize
something is missing after treatment, he says,
sending me home with pocket of pharmacy drugs,
concoctions designed for those who want to live.

ILLUSION OF AN OVERWHELM
By John Amen
NYQ Books
89 Pages
$14.94 Paperback
ISBN: 978-1630450489
To order: https://www.amazon.com/Illusion-Overwhelm-Jon-Amen/dp/1630450480/ref=sr_1_1?s=books&ie=UTF8&qid=1519162655&sr=1-1&keywords=illusion+of+an+overwhelm

Beautifully designed and elegantly produced, this collection by John Amen, *The Pedestal's* founder and editor, is a brilliant linguistic *tour de force*. As in Amen's previous poetry collections, he drives language to the brink and never fails to amaze. Divided into four sections, he begins with "Hallelujah Anima." From "#1:"

> the purpose of desire
> is to propagate desire
> & its concomitant recoil:
> ambivalence is truth.
>
> … A man drags his secrets from dream to dream,
> secrets that drag him through a hundred skins.
> Anima says give them to me,
> but she never takes them,
> & I just can't let them go.

Four prose poems follow this "opening salvo" in the "Anima" section, and each does exactly what prose poems are supposed to do. The imagery is fresh and startling and gives a nod to the surreal.

The second section, "The American Myths," offers profound insights into its subject and even conjures up Dante's Beatrice in #15:

> … It's torture
> to study a Beatrice, not that you crave what you see, rather:
> you see nothing at all. Give up your keys & swinging doors:
> the bed you crash by night, maybe by morning you remain.

In the third section, "My Gallery Days," Amen examines self and soul and ends the sections with these lines from #23:

> … We fled ourselves
> for a season, clutching our self-portrait,
> we were ghosts long before we knew it.

The fourth section, "Portrait of Us," again emerges through surprising imagery and the surreal. The shortest of the sections, this one is strongly relational and concludes:

> Though all the names are forgotten,
> this remains: we uttered what the creator can't;
> the one music it needed from us,
> this is what we give.

The poems in this collection make you think (whether you want to or not). You spin between the physical and the metaphysical, you pass through the world at unusual angles, and you reconcile the dramas of self and soul in unexpected and challenging ways. This is a profound and wildly creative collection that you'll want to read again and again.

DANTE'S UNINTENDED FLIGHT
By Emily Vogel
NYQ Books
80 Pages
$14.95 Paperback
ISBN: 978-1630450465
To order: https://www.amazon.com/Dantes-Unintended-
Flight-Emily-Vogel/dp/1630450464/ref=sr_1_1?s=books&ie=
UTF8&qid=1519165306&sr=1-1&keywords=Dante%27s+U
nintended+Flight

This collection of linked prose poems by the supremely gifted Emily Vogel moves between the domestic and far-reaching worlds that men and women share in their relationships to one another. Vogel's use of language and form is always astonishing and compelling, always rich in metaphor and meaning. She is a true master of prose poem form who infuses her poems with complete sentences and deliberate fragments, intense imagery, the language of dreams, and a more-than-casual courtship with the surreal.

Vogel's "man" and "woman," her "little girl," and her "little boy" (as she calls them in these poems) speak of family and of the spirit-seeking elation and despair that we call life. These poems are luminously unique and fiercely from the heart.

Woman dreams at night of the self, projected, and dies. The rooms are dark like a slow dream. People are asking questions as to where they find woman's things so as to remember her by. There is a quiet fountain running in the hallway. But woman is not woman. Woman is the self that she longs to be and man is touching her cheek. ... She watches the birds cut through the fog and tries to fathom why she is body standing in the actuality of non-dream. She is non-dream and in waking she is a rude apparition. Man is eternally awake and occupying rooms like a differential. Little girl sleeps and dreams and does not know what a dream is.

There is an immediacy in these prose poems that draws the reader into them and won't let go. There is also attention to the ordinary that is transformed into words in the most extraordinary ways. It's as if Vogel is a present-day alchemist who transmutes the lead of language into gold. I recommend this book without reservation—it's a must-have for your library!

COAT THEIF
By Jeffrey Davis
Saint Julian Press
74 Pages
$9.00 Paperback
ISBN: 978-0996523134
To order: https://www.amazon.com/Coat-Thief-Jeff-Davis/
dp/0996523138/ref=sr_1_1?s=books&ie=UTF8&qid=15191
68374&sr=1-1&keywords=coat+thief

Coat Thief is a collection of luminous meditations that perfectly embraces the idea that all poems should have obvious subject matter, as well as content that is unwritten and left for the reader to discern. Most of these poems begin in the ordinary (and beautiful) things of daily life and move into larger, more universal, concerns (earthly and spiritual alike).

Davis has perfected the blending of wisdom and discovery in these poems. Consider this excerpt from "A Series of Small Wonders:"

> Sometimes it is enough to cradle cracks
> of light from the wood stove window
>
> and from that tiny opening that quakes
> all of it new again and again.

These poems are focused and powerful, driven by commanding imagery and buttressed by craftsmanship that is confident and clear. It's as if Davis's poems emerge into, not merely out of our relationship with the natural world and with one another. Along with keen observation and adeptness of line and image, these poems are both thoughtful and thought-provoking. With quiet elegance and meditative beauty, they grace us and bless us with a purity that seeks and finds a quiet place in our hearts that rests with the Divine. From "Heron:"

> here on the limb
> our wings and head fold in
> our form a long closed eyelid
> the quiet confidence of being alone
> waves in our wake

Tiferet

     here in pale light
     here on water
     here on air
     heron

Reading these poems offers a sense of being (as Davis phrased it in "Insomnia") "stupendously awake in the dark." I read and reread these poems with deep gratitude—you will find in them world and spirit, generosity, and the far-reaching insights of love. This is a collection you'll come back to over and over again.

Contributors

SANDRA ERBE (COVER ART)

Artist Sandra Erbe (www.sandraerbe.com) discovered her ability to translate a positive artistic spirit onto canvas following a personal tragedy in 2007. She believes that a creative spirit is present in each of us and encourages everyone to look within. Tapping into one's creative spirit is a great way to open up new channels for problem-solving and stress relief. Sandra's Fluid Art classes allow students to explore their own artistry   often for the first time ever. Sandra can be contacted at sandra@ sandraerbe.com for commissions or archival quality giclées.

GAYLE BRANDEIS (EDITOR-IN-CHIEF)

Gayle is the author of *Fruitflesh: Seeds of Inspiration for Women Who Write* (HarperOne), *Dictionary Poems* (Pudding House Publications), and the novels *The Book of Dead Birds* (HarperCollins), which won Barbara Kingsolver's Bellwether Prize for Fiction of Social Engagement, *Self Storage* (Ballantine), *Delta Girls* (Ballantine), and *My Life with the Lincolns* (Henry Holt Books for Young Readers), which received a Silver Nautilus Book Award and was chosen as a state-wide read in Wisconsin. Two books are forthcoming in 2017, a memoir, *The Art of Misdiagnosis: Surviving My Mother's Suicide* (Beacon Press) and a collection of poetry, *The Selfless Bliss of the Body* (Finishing Line Press). Her work has appeared in such publications as Salon, The Rumpus, The Nation, and The San Francisco Chronicle; one of her essays was listed as "Notable" in Best American Essays 2016. She was named a Writer Who Makes a Difference by The Writer Magazine. She served as Inlandia Literary Laureate from 2012-2014 and currently teaches at Sierra Nevada College and the low residency MFA program at Antioch University, Los Angeles.

CHRISTINE VALTERS PAINTNER

Christine Valters Paintner is an American poet and writer living in Galway, Ireland. Her poems have been published in *The Galway Review, Boyne Berries, Headstuff, Skylight 47, Crannog, North West Words, Spiritus Journal, Tiferet, Anchor, Presence, ARTS, U.S. Catholic, The Blue Nib*, and *Artis Natura*. Her first collection, *Dreaming of Stones*, will be published by Paraclete Press in 2019. You can find more of her writing at AbbeyoftheArts.com.

Tiferet

JUDITH BARRINGTON

Judith Barrington's *Lifesaving: A Memoir* was the winner of the Lambda Book Award and a finalist for the PEN Award for the Art of the Memoir. She is also the author of *Writing the Memoir: From Truth to Art* and four collections of poetry. She has been a faculty member of the University of Alaska's low-residency MFA Program.

EDWIN ROMOND

Edwin Romond's most recent book is *Alone with Love Songs,* from Grayson Books. He was a public school English teacher for thirty-two years before retiring. He currently works part-time in the poetry division of the Geraldine R. Dodge Foundation, facilitating "Spring and Fountain" groups for New Jersey teachers. He lives in Wind Gap, Pennsylvania, with his wife, Mary, their son, Liam, and their dog, Oscar.

TERI FULLER

Teri Fuller is an M.F.A. Creative Non-Fiction student at Antioch University in Los Angeles, and she is also an Associate Professor of English at Waubonsee Community College in IL. She is an emerging writer, and her work has been published in Lunch Ticket. Her work includes fiction, non-fiction, personal essay, and flash fiction. She lives with her husband and three children outside of Chicago--where far western suburbs meet cornfields.

C.W. BUCKLEY

C.W. Buckley lives and works in Seattle with his family. Corporate by day, Catholic by faith, he's a fourth generation West Coast native whose writing explores geek culture, conscience, faith, and fatherhood. Reading regularly at Easy Speak Seattle in the city's northeast, his work has appeared in *Rock & Sling, Lummox Journal, Poesy Magazine*, and the Bay Area Poets Coalition anthology. His chapbook, *Bluing*, is forthcoming from Finishing Line Press. You can follow him as @chris_buckley on Twitter.

VICTORIA WADDLE

Victoria is an unapologetic reader of banned books, a writer, and a teacher-librarian. She's been published in national literary magazines and anthologies, contributes to Inlandia's "Literary Journeys" column and writes book reviews for her "School Library Lady" blog. She is the mother of three boys.

SIAMAK VOSSOUGHI

Siamak Vossoughi was born in Tehran, grew up in Seattle, and lives in San Francisco. He has had some stories published in various journals, and his collection, *Better Than War,* received a 2014 Flannery O'Connor Award for Short Fiction.

ALLISON SCHUETTE

Allison Schuette is a writer interested in documenting lives in a variety of mediums and genres. An Associate Professor at Valparaiso University, she also co-directs the Welcome Project, an online, digital story collection used to foster conversations about community life and civic engagement. Her written work has appeared in *Michigan Quarterly Review, Gulf Coast Review, Mid-American Review*, and other journals. Schuette has received a Ragdale residency and two NEH grants.

JOANN BERTELO

JoAnn Bertelo spent over thirty years teaching English at a high school in New Jersey. After many nights moonlighting as a poet in various venues throughout the state, she has finally returned to her first true love—writing. JoAnn loves all things beautiful, all things meaningful, all things peaceful, and of course, all things poetic.

ALEX LANG

Alex Lang is a poet, painter, filmmaker and principal at Slang Media Lab. His poems and paintings have appeared in a handful of publications and anthologies. He lives in Altadena, CA with his wife, Liza, their children, Poppy & Shepard, and a couple dogs who think they own the place.

MARTIN MORAN

Martin Moran's previous memoir, *The Tricky Part*, received the 2005 Lambda Belles Lettres Award and a Barnes and Noble Discover Prize. His one-man play of the same name was honored with a 2004 OBIE. His recent play, *All The Rage*, won the 2013 Lortel Award for Outstanding Off-Broadway Solo Show. His writing has appeared in *Ploughshares*, the Pushcart Prize anthology, and *The New York Times*. Moran makes his living as an actor in New York City where he lives with his husband, Henry Stram.

LESLÉA NEWMAN

Lesléa Newman is the author of seventy books for readers of all ages, including the short story collections, *A Letter to Harvey Milk* and *Girls Will Be Girls*, the poetry collections, *I Carry My Mother* and *Lovely*, and the children's books, *Ketzel, The Cat Who Composed* and *Heather Has Two Mommies*. Her literary awards include a Money for Women/ Barbara Deming Memorial Fiction Writing Grant and creative writing fellowships from the National Endowment for the Arts and the Massachusetts Artists Foundation. She has had short stories published in *Lilith Magazine, Persimmon Tree,* and others. From 2008 to 2010 she served as the poet laureate of Northampton, MA. Currently she teaches at Spalding University's low-residency MFA in writing program.

WILLIAM KENOWER

William Kenower is the author of *Fearless Writing: How to Create Boldly and Write With Confidence*, and *Write Within Yourself: An Author's Companion*, and the Editor-in-Chief of Author magazine. In addition to his books he's been published in *The New York Times, Edible Seattle,* and *Parent Map*, and has been a featured blogger for the *Huffington Post*.

RJ JEFFREYS

RJ Jeffreys is a published poet and writer, produced playwright, editor and modern Transcendentalist. He is also the Senior Producer for Tiferet Journal's *Tiferet Talk* interviews live radio show and a Tiferet contributing editor. He lives in a costal town, north of Boston, Massachusetts, where the local, historically abundant literary influences of past and present writers and poets, and the ocean, are a constant source of inspiration for him.

MARCIA KRAUSE BILYK

An avid world traveler, Marcia Krause Bilyk works part-time as spiritual director at a New Jersey residential treatment center for alcohol and drug addiction. Her images have appeared in the *Adirondack Review, Cold Mountain Review, Drunk Monkeys, Brevity,* and *Tiferet* (Autumn, 2014).

ARTHUR SOLWAY

Arthur Solway's poetry and essays have most recently appeared in *TriQuarterly, The Antioch Review, BOMB,* and *Salmagundi*, with forthcoming work in *The London Magazine* and *The Tupelo Quarterly*. He is also a frequent contributor of reviews and cultural essays to *Artforum, Frieze,* and *Art Asia Pacific* magazines. A graduate of the Warren Wilson MFA Program for Writers, he has been based in Shanghai since 2007.

Tiferet

LISA ROMEO

Lisa Romeo is the author of *Starting with Goodbye: A Daughter's Memoir of Love after Loss* (University of Nevada Press, May 2018). Her work has been cited in *Best American Essays: 2016* and published in the *New York Times, O, Brevity, Under the Sun, River Teeth's Beautiful Things, Full Grown People,* and other places. Lisa teaches in Bay Path University's MFA program, and lives in New Jersey with her husband and sons.

CONNY JASPER

Conny Jasper has been involved in the creative arts since childhood and studied fine art in college. She is particularly interested in light, shadows, shapes, colors, patterns, and textures and how these elements interact to create a particular mood or visual experience. Conny had two photographic works in an exhibition at the Hamilton Street Gallery in Bound Brook, NJ, and her piece entitled "The Magnificence of the Water" was sold.

JANE EBIHARA

Jane Ebihara is a retired teacher living in rural North Jersey. She is the author of the chapbook, *A Little Piece of Mourning* (Finishing Line Press, 2014). Her poems have been anthologized in several collections and published in such journals as *Adanna Literary Journal, U.S.1 Worksheets,* and the *Edison Literary Review.*

ILONA FRIED

Ilona Fried writes about awareness practices with a focus on the Feldenkrais Method of Somatic Education. The teachings of Moshe Feldenkrais inspired her to roll out of her comfort zone and into an Aikido dojo. Her blog and links to personal essays can be found at www.ilonafried.com.

LYNN DOMINA

Lynn Domina is the author of two collections of poetry, *Corporal Works* and *Framed in Silence,* and the editor of a collection of essays, *Poets on the Psalms.* She serves as Head of the English Department at Northern Michigan University and also as Creative Writing Editor at *The Other Journal.*

LARAINE HERRING

Laraine Herring's latest book is *On Being Stuck: Tapping into the Creative Power of Writer's Block.* (Shambhala 2016). She's the recipient of the Barbara Deming Award for Women and her work has been nominated for a Pushcart Prize. She directs the creative writing program at Yavapai College. laraineherring.com

MICHELLE ORTEGA

Michelle is a speech-language pathologist in private practice who holistically supports patients of all ages to connect with their voices. She seeks to capture the sacred space of ordinary moments through poetry and photography. A New Jersey native, she often road-trips (near and far) and travels to France with her twenty-something daughter, Tori. Prana and Lucie, her feline fur babies, eat, nap and groom themselves until they return.

DHEEPA R. MATURI

Dheepa R. Maturi is a graduate of the University of Michigan and the University of Chicago. Her work has appeared in *Brevity, Every Day Poems, Tweetspeak Poetry, A Tea Reader, Mothers Always Write, Here Comes Everyone, Flying Island, Branches, Hoosier Lit, Dear America: Reflections on Race*, and *The Indianapolis Review*.

PRISCILLA ORR

Priscilla Orr, author of *Jugglers & Tides* and *Losing the Horizon* from Hannacroix Creek Books, has published in *Southern Poetry Review, Tiferet* and other journals. She's a Geraldine. R Dodge poet and founding Director of the Silconas Poetry Center and *The Stillwater Review*. She lives with Crosby, her spirited terrier.

SUSAN POHLMAN

Susan Pohlman is a freelance writer, writing coach, and writing retreat leader based in Phoenix, Arizona. She is the author of the memoir, *Halfway to Each Other: How a Year in Italy Brought Our Family Home*. Her essays have appeared in a various publications, including *The Washington Times, Homelife Magazine, Guideposts, GoodHousekeeping.com*, and *Raising Arizona Kids*. Visit her website at www.susanpohlman.com.

ELAINE KOPLOW

Elaine Koplow is a retired English teacher and union organizer and currently the Director of the Sussex County Writers' Roundtable, Assistant Copy Editor of The Stillwater Review, and Associate Editor of The Paulinskill Poetry Project. A two-time Pushcart Prize nominee, her poems appear in *Spillway, Edison Literary Review, Wawayanda Review, Exit 13 Magazine, U.S. 1 Worksheets, Journal of New Jersey Poets*, and elsewhere.

RAY CICETTI

Ray Cicetti is a poet living in Mountain Lakes, New Jersey. His poem, "Coming Home," can be found at *The Metaworker* online poetry journal. He is also a Zen teacher and psychotherapist interested in bringing spirit into poetry and the healing arts.

NANCY L. CONYERS

Nancy L. Conyers has been published in Lunch Ticket, The Manifest-Station, Role Reboot, Hupdaditty, The Citron Review, Alluvium, and Unconditional: A Guide to Loving and Supporting Your LGBTQ Child. She lives in Malmö, Sweden.

REG DARLING

Reg Darling lives in Vermont with his wife and cats. When he isn't writing, he paints and wanders in the woods. His essays have been published in *Azure, Backcountry Journal, Cicatrix, Dark Matter Journal, The Dr. T.J. Eckleburg Review, Hellbender Journal, Hoot, Traditional Bowhunter Magazine,* and *Primitive Archer.*

PEGGY JAMES

Peggy Is a documentary photographer who hopes to capture bits of the sacred that can be found in the moments of everyday life. You can find her on Instagram @ MiriamZayneb

TOM PLANTE

Tom Plante was born in New York City. He studied Geography at the University of California, Berkeley, and worked for several newspapers, including *The Berkeley Barb, The Irish Echo,* and *The Courier News.* Tom published *Berkeley Works* magazine (1981-85) and has published the poetry journal *Exit 13 Magazine* since 1988. His recent collection of poems is "*Atlas Apothecary*" (Finishing Line, 2016). Tom lives in Fanwood, New Jersey, with his wife and daughter.

DANIEL MENAKER

Daniel Menaker was a *New Yorker* editor for twenty years and later became Editor-in-Chief of Random House. The author of seven books—three of them among the *Times'* 100 best books of the Year—he has won two O'Henry awards and has written humor, journalism, and essays for many publications.

WRYLY T. MCCUTCHEN

Wryly T. McCutchen is a poet, memoirist, and performer based in Seattle. They're an intimacy witch, level-12 empath, and a tattoo whisperer. They hold an MFA in Creative Writing from Antioch University Los Angeles. You can find more of their poetry in their new collection *My Ugly and Other Love Snarls* as well as in upcoming issues of Foglifter and Wanderer.

ANITA FENG

Major writing awards include a National Endowment for the Arts grant and the Pablo Neruda Prize for poetry. Publications: a cross-genre novel *Sid* and two books of poetry, *Internal Strategies* and *Sadie & Mendel*. Currently, Anita teaches Zen in Seattle, Washington, and works as a ceramic artist making raku Buddhas.

GEORGIANA NELSEN

Georgiana Nelsen has practiced business law for many years, though now considers herself as recovering. She makes sense of the world through reading and writing fiction. Her four children, three grandchildren, two dogs, and one patient husband keep her optimistic. She has been revising three different novels for several years.

KATHARINE COLDIRON

Katharine Coldiron's work has appeared in *Ms., the Rumpus, The Masters Review,* and elsewhere. Full disclosure at kcoldiron.com.

THELMA WURZELBACHER

Dr. Thelma Wurzelbacher, C.PP.S., teaches at an urban community college and volunteers at several nursing homes. She hosts international trainees from many academic settings. She writes poetry, short stories, and essays for publication and currently emphasizes photographs as a way of documenting emotions and characters that are typically overlooked.

LACOYA KATOE

LaCoya Katoe is a teaching artist and educator. She facilitates literature, poetry and writing workshops for teens in underserved communities across the country, and lectures and tutors college students. She received her MFA from Antioch University Los Angeles and is a Voices of Our Nation Arts Foundation fellow.

ADELE KENNY

Adele Kenny's poems, reviews, and articles have been published in journals, books, and anthologies worldwide. Among other awards, she has received poetry fellowships from the NJ State Arts Council and Kean University's Distinguished Alumni Award. Her book, *A Lightness, A Thirst, or Nothing at All* was a 2017 Paterson Poetry Prize Finalist. A former creative writing professor, she is founding director of the Carriage House Poetry Series and has been poetry editor of *Tiferet Journal* since 2006.

LOIS P. JONES

Lois P. Jones has work forthcoming in *New Voices: Contemporary Writers Confronting the Holocaust* (Vallentine Mitchell of London). Some publications include *The Poet's Quest for God* (Eyewear Publishing); *Narrative, American Poetry Journal* and *Tupelo Quarterly.* She received the 2016 Bristol Poetry Prize and the 2012 Tiferet Poetry Prize. Her first collection, *Night Ladder*, is Glass Lyre Press's 2017 Book Award winner.

MARY MAKOFSKE

Mary Makofske's latest books are *World Enough, and Time* (Kelsay, 2017) and *Traction* (Ashland Poetry Press, 2011), the Snyder Award winner. Her poems have appeared in many literary journals nationwide and internationally and in eighteen anthologies. In 2017 she received Atlanta Review's Poetry Prize and the New Millennium Prize. www.marymakofske.com

VIRGINIA CHASE SUTTON

Virginia Chase Sutton's chapbook, *Down River,* has been released. Her second book, *What Brings You to Del Amo,* won the Morse Prize, and will be republished by Doubleback Books. *Embellishments* is her first book and her third is *Of a Transient Nature.* Her poems appeared in *Paris Review, Ploughshares,* and other literary publications, journals, and anthologies.

JOHN AMEN

John Amen is the author of four collections of poetry: *Christening the Dancer* (Uccelli Press, 2003), *More of Me Disappears* (Cross-Cultural Communications, 2005), *At the Threshold of Alchemy* (Presa, 2009), and *strange theater* (New York Quarterly Books, 2015). *The New Arcana*—a multi-genre collaborative work co-written with Daniel Y. Harris—was released by New York Quarterly Books in October 2012. His work has appeared in numerous journals nationally and internationally and been translated into Spanish, French, Hungarian, Korean, and Hebrew. In addition, he has released two folk/folk rock CDs: *All I'll Never Need* (Cool Midget 2004) and *Ridiculous Empire* (2008). He is also an artist, working primarily with acrylics on canvas. Amen travels widely giving readings, doing musical performances, and conducting workshops. He founded and continues to edit *The Pedestal Magazine.*

EMILY VOGEL

Emily Vogel's poetry, reviews, translations, and essays have been published widely, most recently in *The North American Review* and *Omniverse.* She is the author of five chapbooks and three full-length collections, the most recent being "*Dante's Unintended Flight*" (NYQ Books, 2017). She is married to the poet, Joe Weil, and teaches writing at SUNY Oneonta.

JEFFREY DAVIS

Jeffrey Davis equips creatives, entrepreneurs, and business leaders to leverage their ideas into expanding their influence with integrity. His work and research with creative innovators, scientists, and social psychologists offers him leading insights on how creatives flourish in times of challenge and change. He has taught at and is a highly sought after speaker for numerous conferences, universities, and centres. He's author of the book *The Journey from the Center to the Page* (Penguin; Monkfish Publishing) the poetry collections *City Reservoir* (BarnBurner Press) and *Coat Thief* (Saint Julian Press), and other books. He also writes on the science of creativity as a regular contributor to Psychology Today and The Creativity Post. Davis heads up a renegade team of creatives, as a branding consultant, at the Tracking Wonder Consultancy. He lives with his wife and two daughters in a farmhouse in the Hudson Valley of New York.

Donor Honor Roll

$0-$99

Ina RoyFaderman
Kelly Ramsdell
Anna Weber
Catherine Leverenz
Judith Sherrard
Kim Buskala
Laura Melmed
Sandra Dvergsdal
Sharon Ingraham
Steven Bakur
Sean Breckenridge
Emily Rufino
Virginia Schultz
Brad Miller
Charmian Woodhouse
David Fittipaldi
Jennifer Begin
Jessica Segall
Judith Gaietto-Grace
Lisa Jordan
Nancy Schlosser
Pat Whalen
Regina A. Davey
Shirley Mitchell
Carole Newlands
Christopher Niedt
Jennifer Thibodeau
John Edward Hasse
Lawrence Ballon
Margaret Stiassni-Sieracki
Marjorie Swett
Patricia Hoban-Rich
Shannon Lockhart
Jacqueline L. Robinson
Mr. P. Saville

Sarah Toth
Bonnie Coulter
Maureen Meshenberg
Anneliese Schultz
Amy Bartow-Melia
Amy Van Allen
Benjamin Coonley
Bridget A. Nutting
Bruce Goss
David Thibodeau
Helen Woodman
Jack Zellner
John Cioffi
Juliana Jacobson
Kenneth Knapman
Mary Beth Kirchner
Mel Leshinsky
Naresh Chandra Saxena
Tina Minkowitz
Mr K.H. Graser
Karl Francis Segall
Alison Knapman
Word Walker Press
Anonymous
Anne H. Woodworth
Concetta Moore
Raechel Bratnick
Gail Gerwin
Geraldine Miller
Linda Leschak
Melissa Kirkpatrick
Cynthia Keyworth
All Weather Music
Gladys Swan
Michael Orlando Yaccarino

Donor Honor Roll

$0-$99

Talia Carner
Lance Mushung
Linda Stryker
Lori Martinez
Beverly Brodsky
Marcia Slatkin
Thelma Zirkelbach
Michael Fontana
Maria Gillan
Terin Miller
Astrid Fitzgerald
Wendy Wolf
Ami Kaye
Sharleen Leahey, songs4peace
Michael Kosoy
Basil Rouskas
Deena Linett
Dani Antman
Florence Shelso
Diane Bonavist
Miriam Katsikis
Bradford Bedar
Steve Butcher
Julie Maloney
Victoria Kaloss
Jesse Hoffmann
Debra Michels
Jennifer Clements
Ronald Pies
Stephanie Cowell
Alison Morse
Katherine Hauswirth
Dawn Raffel
Joan Daidone

Peter Noterman
Betti Kahn
Mark Hillringhouse
Kathryn Ridall
Karen Bookman Kaplan
Priscilla Orr
Charles DeFanti
Floyd Kemske
Jeanne Larsen
Ava Haymon
Susan Balik
Kathleen Petranech
Ronna Wineberg
Mark P. and Arlyn Miller
Lucinda Gadow
Linda Swanberg
Barbara Adler

Donor Honor Roll

$100-$249

Denise Fleissner
Diane Kresh
John Gray
Karen Adey
Louise Moriarty
Marie Hellinger
Ray Landy
Susan Clampitt
Tobi Watson
Virginia Ricc
Julie Stuckey
Peter Smoluchowski
David Tornabene
Susan Jackson
Michcle Daniel
Lawrence V. Stein

A Spiritual Memoir by Dani Antman

Wired for God, Adventures of a Jewish Yogi is the candid and compelling memoir of Dani Antman's spiritual journey from mystical Judaism through Kundalini Science and back again. With a spiritual practice aimed at the redirection and completion of a challenging Kundalini process related to her Jewish past, Dani experiences a triumphant return to Judaism. For all seekers looking to make spiritual progress and find their own spiritual path.

WIRED FOR

GOD

Adventures of a Jewish Yogi

DANI ANTMAN

www.wiredforgod.com

"A story of an inner journey of self-discovery, profound healing, fierce honesty, and startling transformation. This book . . . inspires us to persevere through every resistance, and let the deepest wisdom of our hearts guide us home."
- Rabbi Shefa Gold, Director of The Center for Devotional, Energy, and Ecstatic Practice

FOSTERING PEACE THROUGH LITERATURE & ART

SUBMIT YOUR WRITING
FOR POSSIBLE PUBLICATION IN TIFERET

We are always on the lookout for well-written, engaging, and hopefully consciousness-raising poetry and prose. Our editors carefully review each submission and selections are chosen for each issue.

Tiferet will be accepting submissions for our annual Writing Contest from MARCH 1, 2018 – JUNE 1, 2018. Awards of $500 are given in each of three categories: Poetry, Fiction, and Nonfiction.

Visit http://tiferetjournal.com frequently for updates on submission dates and guidelines.

SUBMIT YOUR AD

Our readers, fans, followers and friends are interested in writing, spirituality, and promoting tolerance.

If you would like to advertise a product or service that is appropriate and relevant, please contact Lisa at lisa@tiferetjournal.com. She can tell you more about the opportunities available to you in our print and digital issues, newsletter, Facebook and Twitter promotions, radio show—hosting, and more.